# The Absolutely, Positively World's *Worst* Joke Book!

by

Hal Horton

"Absolutely on target! By far the funniest book I have ever read."

*Hal Horton*

"Clearly a sign of comic genius …. may be the only book of jokes you need ever own!"

*Hal Horton*

"Humor that undoubtedly will elevate the spirit. Men of reason cannot but find honor in speaking of these bane witticisms. "

*Baron von Frankenstein*

"Come on, guys. Horton is a lunatic….a loose cannon. He's three pints short of a six-pack. Even his gerbil doesn't trust him."

*Hal's neighbor (name withheld)*

"A high-spirited romp. Cuts to the chase. Comes at you with both barrels blazing. It gave us more joy than anything we have ever known."

*Gomez and Morticia Adams*

"In my 'Inferno' Hell spiraled into seven descending levels of anguish, agony, hopelessness and despair. Had I been aware of this book, I most assuredly would have believed it to be the eighth and most dark and despairing level of all."

*Alighieri Dante*


"Arf"

*Lassie*

# The Absolutely, Positively World's <u>*Worst*</u> Joke Book!

☺ ☻ ☹ ☺ ☻ ☹ ☺ ☻ ☹ ☺
☺ ☻ ☹ ☻ ☹ ☺

by Hal Horton

*To my very tolerant wife and children who were the recipients of so many bad jokes! With love to Judy, David and Amy.*

ISBN-13: 978-1499313536

ISBN-10: 1499313535

Copyright ©2014 by Hal Horton

All rights reserved worldwide. No part of this work may be reproduced in part or whole, in any form or by any means including digital, without written permission from the publisher or author. All incidents, situations, institutions, governments and people are fictional and any similarity to characters or persons living or dead is strictly coincidental.

Laughter is indeed infectious. It is a disease well worth catching.

The late, great comedian, Red Skelton, was a firm believer that humor should never insult, denigrate or hurt anyone. He felt strongly that when a comic resorted to gutter sexual references, foul language, ethnic insults, he was covering up for a lack of talent. His was a profound lesson indeed.

Red Skelton also had incredible comic talent.

Well, readers, I make no pretenses whatsoever that this book displays talent in any form, even *subtle*. It is, after all, the absolutely, positively world's *worst* joke book, not the *best*. It may very well insult your intelligence – and it will use every effort to do so. But it will not slink to any ethnic-bashing, religion-bashing, denigration of women, comic treatment of rape and abuse of any kind, gutter sexual references, foul language, bathroom humor. Imagine that! A "G" rated joke book!

In other words, all those knee-slapping, sidesplitting jokes about body parts, excrement, foul language, shocking sex will be missing. What's left? Really lousy jokes that stand squarely on their own merit.

Hey, let's face it. Sex is ingrained in our lives and there will be some references scattered throughout this book. I certainly hope that it comes across as having been done with class (class?) and speaking to the general silliness that characterizes this whole work.

There is indeed a sharp line between bad humor and humor that is disgusting. In short, this is a book that can *truly* be read in mixed company (mixed *up* company?).

So let your intelligence be insulted. I can assure you that your sensibilities will not.

Hundreds of volumes – perhaps *thousands* of volumes – have been written on humor: analyzing it, teaching it, philosophizing over it, even describing its impact on not only our individual health but on the health of our society. Despite all the agonizing discourse, hand wringing, grunting, chest pounding, no one has ever been able to tell us once and for all what makes a joke good or makes it bad.

Henny Youngman may take the credit for telling probably the world's shortest joke: "Take my wife.....*please!*" This joke has been studied and dissected in books and in college courses on psychology, philosophy and humor across the country. A lot of impact for four little words.

Who has the record for the world's longest joke? Two choices come to mind: my counselor at Boy Scout camp around the evening campfire or a drunken uncle at a wedding reception.

The only thing for sure is that at least at one level a joke results from a surprise twist to a common, everyday event or statement. For this example Henny Youngman again comes to the rescue:

> When a doctor gives a man six months to live, the man complains that he cannot pay his bills. So the doctor gives him another six months.

Enough on philosophy and supposition.

This book will do nothing to shed any more light on the subject. Instead, the reader will at last be given a socially acceptable way to tell a rotten joke!

Let me explain.

Jokes spread like the flu at parties, gatherings of friends, around the water cooler at work. There is always at least one hapless soul compelled by some unknown or even mystical force to tell an anecdote, a story ..... a *joke*. The fateful event inevitably begins with the universal opening line: "Tell me if you've heard this one before." The listeners' defense mechanisms kick immediately into high gear and no matter how funny *you* think the joke is, the battle lines have been drawn and your uphill climb has begun.

Wouldn't it be wonderful if you could wade into the crowd and launch your assault with the perfectly disarming opener: "Hey, everybody. I just read this really great book; it was full of really rotten jokes. Let me share one with you." The audience expectations have been reduced to rock bottom. There will even be relaxed smiles on some faces as the listeners anticipate a truly awful joke, allowing you to cut into the conversation and satisfy your mystical compulsion. Moreover, the audience may even still *be* there after you have finished!

Yes, this book will have performed a true social service.

And you will live to joke another day!

But be forewarned: There is no guarantee that you will not laugh at any of the jokes. You do so, however, totally at your own risk and neither the publisher nor I take any responsibility whatsoever for any joke that genuinely strikes your funny bone.

Any real humor is unintentional and purely coincidental.

The required Public Service product warnings and disclaimers are finished – and so may be your sense of humor after you read this book!

You may now proceed at your own risk.

"…..This book *really* hits the spot!"

*In all likelihood there really is no single world's worst joke. After all, terrible is in the ears of the beholder. But one little anecdote seems to have attained some fame as a front-runner in many bad joke competitions, particularly those held by radio stations. In most cases, writers save the best for last. In this book, with the value system reversed, the worst (best?) shall come first. Here, then, is the leadoff bomb – in the opinion of some, the worst joke ever told.*

*But I must warn you: I fully intend to top this one many times over!*

> A corporal leading his scouting patrol stops on a ridge and calls in his position.
> "Corporal," the Captain asks, "reinforcements are on the way. What do you see from there?"
> Corporal: "There are two divisions of troops and tanks."
> Captain: "You're welcome."

*It isn't difficult to see where this book is leading. So swallow hard, rub your eyes, fasten the seat belt (prevents injury when falling off the couch in disgust) and let's go!*

*Rabbits are a favorite topic and the cuddly creatures have accrued their* **fair** *share of body blows, as the following examples bear witness.*

> Hal: "Joe, how's your cousin doing with his rabbit farm?"
> Joe: "He sold it last week."
> Hal: "Why?"
> Joe: "It was a hare-raising experience."

> Did you hear about the rabbit that one day decided to join organized crime as a protection enforcer? You know how it is: hare today, goon tomorrow!

Gill: "Hey, Bob, why so glum?"

Bob: "The police came this morning and arrested my bunny. It was the third time this month!"

Gill: "Oh, I see. You're having another bad hare day."

*If those tidy morsels haven't made you hopping mad, then you are ready for more.*

A man driving through the countryside hears a thud coming from his right front wheel. Upon stopping his car and getting out, he discovers to his horror that he has run over a little bunny rabbit. Full of remorse at having killed the little critter, he begins to cry. A kindly lady comes out of a nearby house and in a comforting voice says to him, "Don't worry; the stuff in this spray can will make things all better."

She then sprays the poor dead creature over its entire little body.

Suddenly the bunny leaps to its feet and starts hopping around, giving friendly waves to the man and woman. This happy, bouncy scene continues as the bunny hops off into the distance, stopping from time to time to wave at them, his face beaming with happiness.

After the little critter finally disappears, the man turns to the woman and asks in total amazement, "Wha....wha....what the heck is *in* that can, anyway?"

She answers, "Why, it's just my hare restorer and permanent wave."

Then there was the rabbit that saw no reason to live and took its own life. You know how it is: hare today, gone tomorrow!

*There may be more rabbit jokes later – or there may not be. With a world of truly bad humor to explore, we must move on.*

Philosophy: The art of explaining why we should be miserable when we are not.

*And I can predict the following will draw lightning bolts from the current crop of sages and soothsayers:*

> There once was a prophet
> Who found no recourse.
> He took his own life.
> No prophet. No loss.

*And now turning to useless people readily brings us to politicians.*

A freshman senator from a large state goes to the Senatorial Tailor to have his fitting for a new suit. After all, in Washington image is everything and this man was not to be outdone.

The tailor measures wide....measures high....measures low. He then says, "Well, sir, you take a 44 Regular jacket and your pants are a 38 waist by 32 inseam."

"You've got that all wrong, young man. Back home I've been consistently wearing a 48 Long jacket with my pants a 42 waist and a 36 inseam."

The tailor goes around again and comes to the same conclusion he did the first time.

"I'm tellin' ya, son," the senator complains, "you just don't know what you are doing. My tailor has always measured me as a 48 Long with a 42 waist and 36 inseam."

"I'm sorry, sir," the tailor replies. "I guess you just aren't as big a man around here as you are at home."

With the current trends in presidential politics the entrance music for the president will soon be changed to "Hail to the Thief."

*And complaining about politicians allows us to gravitate to other country's leaders.*

"To arms! To arms," shouted the king. "All I have is *two* arms!"

If Tom Thumb were to become a king, his people would live by rule of Thumb.

When Golda Meir [pronounced my-ear], the Prime Minister of Israel, finally met with Gamal Abdel Nasser, the President of Egypt, in the Fall of 1967, he spread his arms and exclaimed, "Golda Meir!"
She shot back, "Gamal, my foot!"

Then there was the surfboard king who took over a small South American "banana republic."
His first official order of business was to hang ten.

After decades of turmoil a new leader emerged in the same "banana republic." The new leader took his stance on the balcony overlooking the main city square and made his proclamation to the anxious people below.

"For years," he shouted, "we have had a leader come forward and pass many, many bills. Soon you the people would get fed up and there would be a coup [pronounced coo]. Then the new leader would pass many, many more bills and again you the people would rise up and there would be a coup."

He gave a long look around the square and then announced, "As your leader, I promise to stop all this billing and couping!"

The Third World revolutionary's favorite song: Grenade-a [Granada].

*As we scout through Third World republics we inevitably come to Fidel Castro, who at this writing had been the world's currently longest lasting leader. (It is bad form to date a book this way, but what's wrong with bad form complementing bad humor?)*

Castration: what results when you make fun of Fidel's manhood.

Infidel: where John F. Kennedy tried to have poison placed.

Cuba: a box with six equal sides.

Fidel Castro was happy over his country's leadership in sugar production until his minister of defense warned about unrest at home.
"What problem can there be?" Castro intoned. "My people seem to be happy."
"Yes, Generalissimo; but they are all raising cane!"

Then there was the fellow who left Cuba, came to the United States, married and raised kids. It is chronicled in the book and movie "Juan Mann's Family."

*Let us move on now into the general areas of poor humor and let the good (?) times roll!*

Man at pool side to lifeguard: "Who is that monstrously huge blob of a man floating out there in the middle of the pool? Geez, he is about as big as a land mass!"
Lifeguard: "That guy? Oh, that's Norman. You know what they say, 'Norman is an island.'"

Camelot: A place where you can buy a used camel.

Party guest to the host: "Boy, people here must think I am some kind of a deity."

Host: "Why do you say that?"

Guest: "When I came through the door several people turned around and said, 'My God, what are you doing here?' "

A motorist is caught speeding. The police officer writes out the citation and hands it to him.

Motorist: "Officer. What's this?"

Policeman: "That's a ticket. You get three of those and you get a bicycle."

Dandruff: Mr. Druff's full name.

A motorist careens around the corner, goes through a red light and travels off at great speed. A police officer takes off in hot pursuit. After the chase ends the policeman demands to see the motorist's license.

Policeman: "In addition to everything else it states here on your license that you are supposed to be wearing glasses."

Motorist: "Well, you see, officer, I have contacts."

Policeman: "I don't care who you know. You're still getting a ticket."

Then there was the man who lost a drag race. The poor fellow was in the lead, but he had a high heel shoe blowout 20 yards before the finish line.

And speaking of cars [???]. What would you get if you painted every automobile in America pink? A pink car nation.

Dandelion: Ralph T. Lion's brother.

"When Hal Horton told me he was gonna put me in his next book, I didn't think he meant it *literally* ...."

    The little pussy cat was trotting down the sidewalk one sunny afternoon, when he passed under a painter's ladder.
    As bad luck would have it, the painter dropped his can of blue paint and it spilled all over the little kitty. A few blocks down the street, the now sad kitten met a friend.
    Friend: "How come you don't look happy?"
    Kitty: "That's because I'm feline blue."

    A friend of mine sent me a male cat from Mainland China. I sent it right back. I didn't want any Peiping Toms around the house.

Then there was the termite who went into a night club and asked, "Where is the bar tender?"

At a cocktail party two men meet and start discussing their occupations.
First Man: "I am an architect. I have been in charge of most of the major construction projects in this city and county. What do you do?"
Second Man: "I am a cartoonist. I do a comic strip."
First Man: "Oh, good. Take off your clothes. I need a good laugh."

Dandelion: a nattily dressed lion.

A man goes to a psychiatrist. "Doc, you've got to help me. I think I'm a horse."
Psychiatrist: "Can you come back tomorrow?"
Man: "But, why, Doc?"
Psychiatrist: "I have a ten dollar bet on you tonight in the sixth race."

Herb: "Why did you throw that lighted dynamite stick down the well shaft?"
Ned: "It says on my medicine bottle, 'Shake well before using.'"

A man goes to a psychiatrist. "Doc, you've got to help me. I think I'm a chicken."
Psychiatrist: "Great! I think I'm a fox!"

If an athlete can catch athlete's foot, does an astronaut get missile-toe?

A man goes to a psychiatrist. "Doc, I think I'm a dog." The psychiatrist feels the man's nose.

"Well, your nose is cold, so you must be healthy," the doctor comments.

"Hey, I'm serious, Doc. This is no laughing matter."

"O.K., O.K.. Lie down on the couch and we'll talk about it."

"I can't," replied the man, "I'm not allowed on the couch at home."

A man goes to a psychiatrist. "Doc, you've got to help me. I think I'm a chicken."

Psychiatrist: "This is pretty serious. We'll have to start treatment immediately."

Months and months pass and the man continues in his analysis. Finally, the treatment takes hold and the man slowly recovers.

One day the man's wife storms into the psychiatrist's office demanding that the treatments be stopped at once.

"I had no idea you were treating my husband," the wife snaps.

"What's the problem?" the psychiatrist exclaims, "don't you want your husband cured?"

"That's fine for you to say," the wife retorts, "but we need the eggs."

A man goes to a psychiatrist. "Doc, you've got to help me. I think I'm a rooster."

Psychiatrist: "What's the problem with that?"

Man: "*You* try sleeping on a fence post!"

A man goes to a psychiatrist. "Doc, you've got to help me. I think I'm a rooster."

Psychiatrist: "How did this happen?"

Man: "When I was a little kid, I was scared at a cocktail party."

A man goes to a psychiatrist. "Doc, you've got to help me. I think I'm a goose."

Psychiatrist: "I think I can help you."

Man: "Great, Doc. What will I owe you?"

Psychiatrist: "Nothing. But when you molt, can I have the feathers for my pillow?"

The football coach was getting frantic. His team had suffered several key injuries and he was down to just a few good men.

Coach to his field manager: "Tom, who's that guy sitting at the end of the bench?"

Tom: "That's Remmy Ulschearveltamelchiovistz."

Coach: "Good. Send him in. I can finally get even with the sportswriters."

Speaking of athletes, there was the star football player who was awarded his letter and then asked his coach to read it to him.

*How about those cra-a-a-a-zy vampires, folks?*

What is the tallest building in Transylvania? Why, the Vampire State Building, of course.

Helen: "Anything I should know before my date tonight with Count Dracula?"

Ellen: "Never, *never* go necking on the first date."

A vampire walks into a blood bank and meanders over to the service counter.

Receptionist: "U-u-l-p-p! D-d-o you want to donate?"

Vampire: "No-o-o. I vant to take out a loan."

The next day the same vampire takes a seat in the waiting room. At long last the receptionist calls him over.

Receptionist: "O.K., Count, your loan has been approved. Just fill in these forms."

Vampire: "Too late. It is 5:00 and I've got to _fly!_"

Then there was the vampire who bought a computer because it could give him a billion <u>bytes</u>.

Liability: the ability to convincingly not tell the truth.

One fine and sunny day a man was walking into town, enjoying the weather and the sights. When he turned the corner he came across a strange sight: another man was lying in the gutter trying to force himself through the storm grate.

First Man: "Hey, buddy! What the heck are you trying to do?"

Second Man: "Leave me alone! I'm trying to commit sewer side!"

It was a dark and dreary night. Thunder and lightening danced about and the drunk, sizing up his situation, decided to take a shortcut through the cemetery to get home before the rain.

He staggered forward; zigged right and zagged left. Suddenly a drenching rain burst from the clouds.

Dazed drunk and with his vision blurred by the rain the hapless soul fell into an open grave site being readied for the next day.

He tried his best to get out. Each time he got a foothold he would slide back in over the mud. This futile effort continued for another 20 minutes until he finally decided to settle down in the corner and make the best of it.

Meanwhile, a short while later another drunk from the same bar began following the same destiny and decided to take a shortcut through the same cemetery.

He staggered forward; zigged right and zagged left.

Dazed drunk and with his vision also blurred by the rain this second hapless soul fell into the same open grave site. He pulled himself up and slid back down. He pulled himself up again and again slid back down.

Meantime, the first man sat in the darkness watching the second fellow go up....slide down....go up....slide down. Finally the first man got up and went over to him, tapped him on the back and said, "You'll never get out."

He *DID!!!*


On another dark and dreary rainy night the cemetery staff workers were preparing for a dinner reception to be held the next day.

A strapping fellow went to the supply shed to fetch a bag of flour. He took a 50-pound bag, tossed it over his shoulder and started back to the reception hall.

On the way he slid in the mud, lost his footing and dropped the bag of flour into an open grave site.

And the plot thickened.


*We all know that the farmer, that most essential of our citizens, is out standing in his field. So please dig our heaping helping of corn.*


There was the poor hapless farmer whose crop output had always come up short. Finally fortune smiled on him and he had a good year.

"Maw," he exclaimed, "we are growing produce for those automobile manufacturers in Detroit."

"How so, Pa?" she asked.

"Well, that nice fellow down at the bank was glad to see that we had a bumper crop this year."

The hotshot punk was racing his hotrod over the back country roads. Suddenly he heard a big thump as he squealed around a curve.

"Pig!" shouted a farmer standing along the side of the road.

The punk screeched his car to halt, backed up and started screaming at the farmer for yelling that at him.

"Have it any way you want," replied the farmer, " but you still owe me 300 bucks for that pig you hit."

Joe: "Hey, Jim. How's your cousin doing with his farm?"
Jim: "He sold it last week."
Joe: "Why?"
Jim: "He kept having a harrowing experience."

One fine day a farmer decided to plant soybeans. After a few seasons he noticed that the crop was getting smaller, so he decided to rotate crops and he planted melons.

The melons did well. In fact they grew so well that the farmer expanded the growing area further and further each year.

Finally, the melons were being planted everywhere. The farmer was looking for more space for his ever more popular melons. He noticed that the only space left on the farm was his dog pen.

"Well, crops are money," he exclaimed, and he plowed on through the dog pen, dogs and all, to plant more melons.

To his surprise, that year no crop came up at all. The next year was the same sad story and the farmer was nearly destitute. At last, near the end of the season one tiny little plant grew. The farmer gently lifted the plant from the ground singing, with a tear in his eye, "Come to me my melon-collie baby."

Speaking of growing things, a friend of mine went into cancer research because he heard that it was a *growth* industry.

Dandelion: untruths from the mouth of Dan D.

Then there was the civil engineer who put flow sheets on the river bed.

Physicist: an ice cream parlor Soda Jerk.

There was the man who fell into a lens grinding machine and made a spectacle of himself.

And there was the poor fellow who fell into a Xerox copier. When he got out he was beside himself.

Why did the moron throw the clock out the window? Because he *was* a moron.

Hal: "Ginnie, I am the Post Office's ideal."
Ginnie: "What's that?"
Hal: "I am a First Class Male."

Jed: "Why so glum, Ned?"
Ned: "I had a harecut this morning."
Jed: "What's the problem with that?"
Ned: "Now I don't have a rabbit covering third base."

Gertie went outside one fine day to mow her lawn. Unknown to her, little Peetie, her parakeet, had escaped from his cage.
Gertie began mowing, cutting flowing swaths across her lawn. Meanwhile, little Peetie landed in the grass and started foraging for seeds, unaware of the approaching lawnmower.
Suddenly there was a loud chirp and feathers scattered in all directions. Gertie began sorrowfully gathering Peetie from his many

locations as her neighbor was walking by.

The neighbor stopped and asked Gertie what she was holding.

"Shredded Tweet," she replied.

The mighty oak dropped its seeds and one little acorn took root far from its mother.

The little seedling looked around and around and could see nothing but rocks and grass. The little plant wondered, "What am I? A rock? A blade of grass?"

As time passed the little sprout grew tall enough to see the trees nearby and it wondered about its identity even more.

Finally, after a rain shower the seedling saw its reflection in a puddle by its base and it looked up at the forest and back down at the reflection.

Suddenly it exclaimed, "Geometry."

A man walked into a blood bank to donate his fair share. After the procedure he wandered into the donors' reception room to rest. While he was sitting an Indian chief came in and sat down next to him.

Man: "I can't help noticing your fine headdress and clothes. Are you a full-blooded Indian?"

Indian: "No, I'm one pint short."

And speaking of ethnic backgrounds, I knew a man who was half scotch and half water.

When playing cards with company, be sure to never play Pinochle with an elephant. Every time you place a card down he is liable to trumpet.

Then there was the "banana republic" dictator who thought that he was a Big Wheel because he operated at three revolutions per week.

A woman went on a vacation to the same "banana republic." While she was seeing the sights she met the esteemed Generalissimo (the same said dictator), who honored her with an audience with him.

Woman: "You certainly have a lovely country here. What is your country's number one sport?"

Dictator: "It is, of course, Bull Fighting."

Woman: "Oh, isn't it revolting?"

Dictator: "No, that is the number two sport."

A husky bodybuilder walked into the Circus Personnel Office to apply for a job.

Personnel Manager: "What kind of work do you want?"

Man: "I'm a human cannonball."

Personnel Manager: "Excellent. We need men of your caliber."

The world's three greatest lies:
    The check is in the mail.
    I'll call you tomorrow.
    I love you.

A priest, a minister and a rabbi were playing cards in the basement of the church. When they heard the Archbishop coming down the steps, they hastily put the cards away and pretended that nothing had been going on.

Unswayed by the serene scene displayed before him, the Archbishop bellowed to the priest, "Father, were you playing cards down here?"

Priest: "Oh, no. Your Reverence, I would not defile the good name of this church by doing such a deed."

Archbishop, turning to the minister, "Pastor, how about you? Were you playing cards down here?"

Minister: "Certainly not, Your Reverence. I, to, have too

much respect to defile the good name of this church by doing such a deed."

Archbishop, addressing the rabbi, "And you, Rabbi? Were you playing cards?"

Rabbi: "With whom?"

Why did the duck cross the road? Because he was tied to the chicken.

Why did the duck cross the road? It was because of the union seniority system: He bumped the chicken.

A retiree joined a retirement community and settled into his lovely apartment overlooking the golf course.

After a few days he found himself bored to tears, so he went out to meet the people in the community. As luck would have it he came across Fred, his old high school chum.

Fred: "Well, I'll be darned. Bob! I can still recognize you after all these years." The two struck up a conversation and soon Fred invited Bob to the weekly social gathering.

At the social hall Fred began introducing Bob around. Suddenly a man sitting a few tables away stood up and shouted out, "Twenty three!" People began laughing, a few people only smiled and some people even booed.

"What's happening here?" Bob asked his friend.

Fred: "Well, you see, Bob, we are all old-timers here. As you know there are no new jokes, just new audiences; well, we all know all of the jokes by heart. To make things easier we have assigned a number to each joke and so when the spirit moves someone, he or she can just stand up and shout out a number. We all know the joke, so we can respond to it as we wish."

The night wore on and people continued to stand up and shout

out numbers. Sometimes the crowd roared with laughter; sometimes laughter was mixed with hisses, and so on.

There was a lull in proceedings, when a man near the back of the room stood up to take his turn.

"Watch this, Bob," Fred whispered, "this man tells our favorite joke." The man then blurted out, "Seventeen!"

The building shook with the resulting laughter. Some people were actually in tears they were laughing so hard. Fred looked at Bob and said, "I guess we're all going to call it a night. Be sure you come back next week."

At the next weekly social Bob and Fred sat together again. And again the number calling brought on the usual audience responses.

Bob waited most of the evening, building his courage to take his turn at telling a joke.

Finally, Bob was ready. He stood up and shouted out, "Seventeen."

The entire room fell silent. People cast icy stares at Bob and began to leave. Fred also got up to leave. Frantically, Bob grabbed at Fred's arm and asked him, "What happened? I thought that was their all-time favorite joke?"

Fred glared at Bob and hissed, "Some people can tell 'em and some people can't."

How does an elephant play piano? By tickling his ivories.

How can you tell where an elephant has traveled? By the stickers on his trunk.

Sign on Psychiatrist's door: "Deposit your head here by 8:00 A.M. I will shrink it and have it back to you by 5:00 P.M."

Salvador Dali, the famous eccentric painter, spent most of his life avoiding meeting Louis Armstrong. He was afraid that Louis Armstrong would say, "Well hello-o-o-o-o, Dali!"

Those who follow baseball may remember the three great baseball stars Mattie Alou [pronounced a-loo], Fillip Alou and Jesus Alou. Two played for the San Francisco Giants at the same time.

What baseball fans do not know is that there was a fourth brother who was even better than the other three *combined*. His name was Roberto. He was a star among stars.

Roberto resisted all attempts to be coerced into trying out for the Major Leagues. He was well aware that stardom was assured for him. But he was deathly afraid that every time he came to bat the crowd would shout, "Bob Al-o-o-o-o-o."

Alas, after long negotiations and hard bargaining, the County Zoo purchased a Roovil, that rarest of all of the world's creatures.

Just as Roovil were not cheap to buy, they were equally as expensive to feed. In fact, the only diet the critter could exist on in captivity was the special combination of paper, ink and fillers that was contained in the US currency.

"This is plain ridiculous," the Zoo manager screamed at his buyer. "How in the blazes could you have pulled such an idiotic stunt! There must be other food that beast will eat. Our plans are to purchase two more Roovil; the solution must be found."

Try as they might, the Zoo personnel could find no alternative to money. The critter certainly had a rich diet.

"All right," the Zoo manager screamed again, "if we have to feed that Roovil money, let us at least keep the denominations small."

The feeding program commenced in earnest with a shipment of two barrels of one dollar bills.

Growth of the Roovil was fast and the hunger needs grew even faster – much faster. Soon the Zoo was feeding $5's, then $10's, on to $100's.

The Zoo manager contacted the president of the company that sold him the critter. "Certainly, there must be some twist of fate here. This money need must be unique to the beast that *we* bought, isn't it?" the Zoo manager asked the company president.

"Oh, no," retorted the president, "everyone knows that money is the eat of all Roovil."

Dandelion: in other words Dan D. is not standing up.

If a duke is called His Lordship, is his wife called Her Battleship?

*Speaking of battleships, government secrecy can be carried to an utter extreme as this next story illustrates.*

One day the crew of the Navy's most decorated battleship received a mystery visitor – a man in a plain dark suit, wearing dark glasses and carrying a large black suitcase.

He approached the ship's admiral and told him, "I have been sent by the top inner most secret operatives of the CIA. to perform a most classified experiment onboard this ship. If you do not want me to bring the President of the United States down on your neck I request that I be allowed complete privacy while I prepare the test device."

"What is the nature of your work?" the Admiral asked the stranger.

"I am a K.U.S.H. maker. K.U.S.H. is the absolutely most secret project the Defense Department is engaged in and I cannot tell you more," he replied.

Not one to go against high command, the Admiral granted the stranger a very private stateroom wherein the mystery man delved immediately into his work.

The months at sea passed slowly as the Admiral wondered constantly what his visitor was doing. The crew was growing more and more restless out of concern for their own safety. Just short of the mutiny point, the man emerged with his large case in tow.

"Admiral, I need two of your most capable men to aid me in completing my test," the stranger declared.

The Admiral obliged and the men brought the case to the Starboard side of the ship and placed it against the railing.

"Open the gate," the mystery man demanded. The gate was opened.

"Push the case forward," the man further demanded.

The two crewmen pushed the case forward and it dropped into the water: *k-u-s-s-s-s-h-h-h-h!*

Donnybrook: marriage between Brooke Shields and Donny Osmond.

Eyeglasses give you foresight.

If the leader of Russia used to be called the Czar and his wife was the Czarina, were their children Czardines?

A man goes to his doctor. "Doc, every time I lift my arm my shoulder hurts like crazy. What should I do?"

"Don't lift your arm," the doctor told him. "That'll be $50."

Holy smoke! The church is on fire!

Chemistry lesson from the radical 1960's: If you are not part of the problem, you are part of the solution. If you are not part of the solution, you are part of the precipitate.

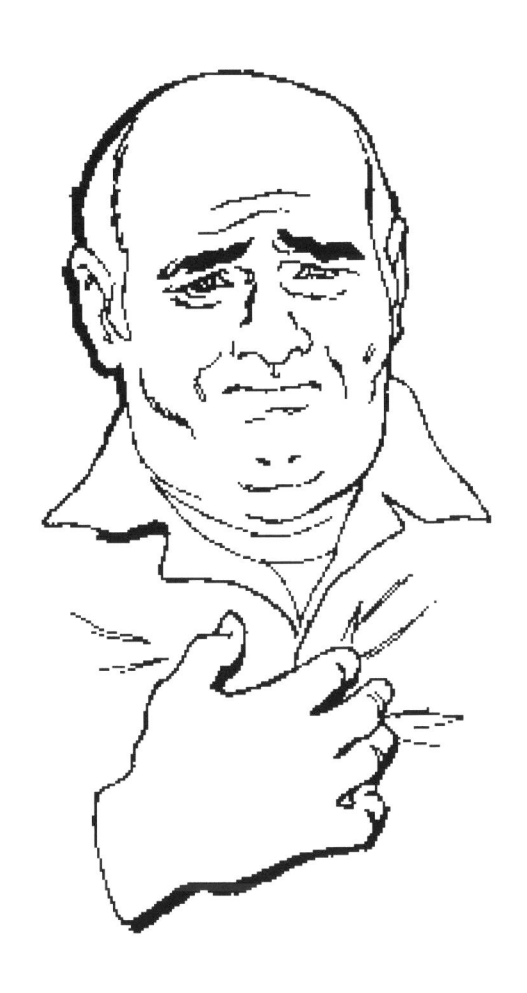

"I can't believe it .... I thought I just saw you smile .... must've been gas bubbles."

Benny lived a quiet life and kept mostly to himself. When he began growing his beard his friends, and especially his girlfriend, were concerned. But Benny continued to grow his beard without even so much as trimming one hair. His beard grew longer and longer until it finally reached its maximum length – three feet!

"Benny, for Pete's sake, please, please shave," his girlfriend implored him.

"I can't," Benny replied quietly, "for as sure as I am standing here before you, I know that as soon as I shave, I will die."

His friends thought that he was crazy and one-by-one they left him. Before long his girlfriend gave him the ultimatum: shave or lose her, too.

Poor Benny went into the bathroom and began shaving. Sure enough, as soon as the last whisker was trimmed, Benny fell over dead.

His girlfriend was heartsick. She followed Benny's wishes and had him cremated.

The moral of the story: A Benny shaved is a Benny urned.

I sat by the Lady at tea.
It was not what it ought to be.
Her rumblings internal were simply infernal,
And everyone thought it was me.

During World War I the Doughboys were fighting a particularly brutal battle. During the fighting one of the soldiers came across a strange bird. Wondering what it was he called his commander over during a lull in the fighting. "Why, that's a rari, a particularly rare bird and very valuable," the commander said.

With the battle over and his troops victorious, the commander lead his troops on to the next confrontation, with the rari in tow as a good luck omen.

But, alas, the rari, like the famed Roovil, grew at an incredible rate. Soon the troops were spending much of their time caring for the now monstrous bird. It became increasingly more difficult to watch the bird and fight battles at the same time.

"That bird has become a major liability," the commander declared one day to the soldier who had found it. "You must shoot it!"

The soldier was greatly saddened by the prospect of killing the creature that he had helped to save. The commander prevailed, however, and three men were assigned the task of killing the bird, with one of the guns loaded with blanks so that no one would actually know who did the killing.

Out of view of the commander the soldier hatched a plan. The bird had never been seen flying, but it was, after all, a bird.

"Let's move him over to that cliff over there and push him over and see if he flies," the soldier schemed. "In that way we have at least a chance of saving his life." They all agreed.

When they got to the cliff, the three looked down. It was an enormous cliff, seemingly over 1000 feet high.

One of the other men looked down over the cliff, looked at the bird and complained, "I don't know. It's a long way to tip a rari."

The football coach was disheartened at the unusually small fan turnout during the season. He bought a dozen pigs and brought them along with the team to the next game.

"Why did you bring all these pigs along," the team captain asked him.

The coach replied, "We needed a rooting section."

After the season was over the same coach found himself burdened with a dozen pigs. He packed them into his truck and headed into the city.

A policeman saw the truck loaded with pigs and pulled it over. "Where are you going with all those pigs?" the policeman asked the coach.

The coach replied, "I'm looking for a porking place."

A man was transporting penguins to the local zoo. While out on the highway his truck broke down, stranding him in the middle of nowhere. Concerned for the safety of his cargo, he began waving cars down for help.

A second man, driving a large pickup, pulled over and offered his assistance.

The first man said, "Fella, I have a dozen penguins in my truck and I was headed to the zoo, when my truck broke down. Your pickup is big enough; could you do me a big favor and take these penguins to the zoo for me. I'll give you $100."

The second man agreed. The penguins waddled up onto his pickup and he drove off. About an hour later the first man received roadside service and his truck was put back in operation.

"I think I'll drive to the zoo and make sure everything is all right with those penguins," he said to himself.

About a mile from the zoo he saw the second man walking along the road with the twelve penguins waddling behind him in a straight line.

"Hey, buddy," the first man shouted, "I thought I told you to take those penguins to the zoo!"

"I did that," the second man replied, "but I had some money left over so now we're going to the movies."

Then there was the monster that joined the convent. He was a creature of habit.

The young hotshot had been caught speeding once too often and he was determined to do something about it. Reform? Not this guy. Instead, he bought a supercharged, retrofitted Ferrari with 5-speed overdrive and a top speed of 185 MPH.

The day after he picked up his new machine, he began cruising the roadway at 70 MPH, looking for his nemesis. As he rounded the next curve, there was the officer in the usual spot. Mr. Hotshot hit the accelerator pedal and squealed off.

Sure enough the motorcycle cop set off in hot pursuit. Our hotshot was ready. Just as the officer was within striking distance, Mr. Hotshot hit the accelerator pedal and the car blazed away out of reach.

The punk hotshot was in his glory. He baited the motorcycle cop time and again. Each time the officer was within reach, the Ferrari would blaze off out of sight.

On the third day of this ridiculousness, Mr. Hotshot decided to really give the motorcycle cop a show. Just as the officer closed in, the young brat slammed down on the accelerator pedal, hurtling the Ferrari into hyperspace. In no time the sports car was cruising at 170 MPH.

The brat turned around and began looking for the officer, but he was nowhere in sight. Suddenly, Mr. Hotshot saw the officer lying in a ditch with the motorcycle resting about 75 feet away. He pulled over to find out what happened.

"You see," said the officer, "the last time you took off, I thought that my motorcycle had stopped and so I got off."

Have you ever seen two giraffes necking?

Have you ever seen two octopuses walking down the beach arm-in-arm, arm-in-arm, arm-in-arm, arm-in-arm, arm-in-arm and arm-in-arm?

Why are elephants hard to understand? Because they talk in truncated sentences.

How do you stop a charging elephant? Take away his credit card.

Bill: "My cousin was captured recently. I couldn't believe it. They say he killed forty people! The County Prosecutor says it is guaranteed that he'll get the electric chair."
Will: "The more power to him."

The hillbilly was elated to find out that his son had been accepted to the big university down state.

"Ma, Jeb is gonna go off and get himself an education. And he tells me he's gonna learn some brand newfangled way to use a gun."

"How so, Pa?" Ma asked.

"He said he was gonna be studying some of that there dadburned trigger-nometry."

Dandelion: a common, yellow-flowered herb related to chicory. (Hey, they can't *all* be funny!)

Boyfriend: "Gee, Helen. you must have teased your hair."
Girlfriend: "Oh, you noticed!"
Boyfriend: "Yeah, it's having a terrible revenge."

Boyfriend: "Hey, Helen, you must have been eating bullets."
Girlfriend: "Why do say that."
Boyfriend: "Your hair is growing out in bangs."

The three-time murderer was asked what he would do if he could do his life all over again.

Murderer: "I, uh, would, uh, like, you know, to, uh speak betterer than I do."

"Well," the warden answered, "you will get your wish. The State is going to offer you electrocution lessons."

The murderer was asked by his friends if he could hang out with them that night.

"I can't," he replied, "I'm on a killer schedule."

My car was so slow, it's 0 – 60 MPH acceleration was measured on a calendar.

I like bananas because they have a peel.

She looked like a million dollars! All green and wrinkled!

The hound dog was trotting along the sidewalk when he came upon a lovely poodle.
"Hi, there," the hound asked her, "what's your name?"
"Fifi," she answered, "and what is yours?"
"I not sure," he replied, "near as I can tell it's Down Boy."

The visitor to Paris could not believe his eyes. The enormity of the structure before him filled his vision and left him dazed.
"What is that monstrous structure," he asked his friend. "Is that what they call the Eye-full Tower?"
The famous heart transplant surgeon was in town for a lecture. The curiosity seekers came out of the woodwork.
The questions flew left and right and the surgeon handled all with aplomb. One questioner momentarily stumped him, when he asked, "You have said that the heart must be removed from the donor very soon after death. How can you be sure that the patient *is* dead when the heart is removed?"
"I can assure you," the surgeon replied, "that when the heart is removed, the patient is most assuredly dead."

Why was the little ceramic sculpture so glum? He found out that first he was going to be fired and then they were going to hang him.

Jed: "I went to a bakery that sells calypso bread."
Ned: "What do you mean?"
Jed: "All of the breads are a day old, a day-ay-ay old."

Octagon: what you say when your octopus has run away from home.

The old sea captain was renowned far and wide for his enormous skill at navigating in both good weather and bad. His sixth sense guided his ships time and again through even the most treacherous shoals.

Every morning when the captain woke up, he went to the huge oak desk in his stateroom, opened the second drawer and took out a little brass box. Upon opening the box he would remove a piece of paper, unfold it and look at it intensely for about five full minutes. Then he would neatly fold the paper back up, replace it in the box and put the box back in his desk.

This routine had been observed by all of his crews dating back to the earliest memory of his oldest ship's mate – more than 39 years!

Nobody had ever asked the old captain what it was that he read, but this routine had vexed all of the crews that had ever served under him.

One day, the old captain took sick and retired to his stateroom. The ship was not under his command for the first time in his career. The stress of not controlling the ship's destiny finally took its toll and the great old captain passed away.

After all of the fitting and proper ceremonies were held, the entire crew made a frantic rush to the old captain's stateroom and to the famous brass box.

All held their breath anxiously while the First Mate removed the box from the desk and opened it. He removed the paper, unfolded it and stared in amazement at the contents.

"What does it say? What does it say?" the other crew members cried out.

The First Mate read the note aloud: "Starboard is right; port is left."

Polygon: what you say when your parrot has flown away from home.

A young couple decided to have dinner at a restaurant. After a long discussion, they decided on Ho's Szechuan House.

At the end of dinner came the fortune cookies. When they opened theirs, both messages read, "Help! I am trapped in the kitchen of a Chinese Restaurant!"

Teacher to student in social studies class: "If you were the leader of Ethiopia in 1945, who would you be?"

The student thought and thought, and then he thought some more. All to no avail. Finally, the teacher said sternly, "You are stalling."

The student replied, "Wasn't he the leader of *Russia?*"

J. Edgar Hoover was not only the head of the FBI ..,. he invented the vacuum cleaner; and then he really cleaned up!

The old Texas town offered fine frontier living and the right combination of outdoor spaciousness and big town excitement. So when the drifter wandered into town, he decided that this was the place for him to settle.

His first stop after settling into his room at the Inn was a visit to the local saloon. Once inside he struck up a friendly conversation with the bartender. After they got to know each other, the bartender offered him a job. "This town has been growing and I can sure use the help," the bartender said.

The drifter accepted immediately, delighted at having landed a job so soon after arriving in town.

The bartender then gave him some guidelines: "You'll see the usual fights, there will be brawls and you'll get an occasional 'friendly' shoot-out, and you'll have the usual supply of rowdy drunks. But one thing I must warn you about. When you hear anyone – and I mean *anyone* – shouting 'Big John is a-comin',' you run like the dickens. You get as far away as fast as possible."

The weeks passed and the drifter saw just what the bartender had told him. There were the brawls and occasional "friendly" shoot-outs. There was the usual supply of rowdy drunks.

One day it happened. A frantic, almost hysterical cowboy came running into the saloon shouting "Big Jo-h-h-h-h-n is acomin'!"

The saloon emptied out with a wild mob rush of people. The drifter tried to get out, but the rushing crowd knocked him down time and again. He staggered to his feet and started to leave, but at the door he saw the most incredible sight he had ever known.

There before him was the most monstrously huge man he had ever seen. This was a man of gargantuan proportions. He had come riding in on a buffalo, dragging a mountain lion in tow. Dismounting from the buffalo, he glared at his animals and told them to stay put. They cowered in submission.

The drifter scurried back into the saloon as the huge man entered, swiping both saloon doors off their hinges with one sweep of his enormous arm. When the behemoth got to the bar, he sat down on four stools and demanded service. "Barkeep! Get me a whiskey!" his voice thundered.

The drifter handed him a gallon bottle and the titan bit the top off and sucked out the contents in three seconds.

The drifter asked him, "C-c-c-c-an I g-g-g-get y-y-you another one?"

"No time!" roared the colossus, "Big Joh-h-h-h-n is acomin!"

Mushroom: room for lovers.

Mushroom: room where only cornmeal mash is served.

Mushroom: classroom where the command to lead an Alaskan dog team is taught.

Szechuan: a form of Chinese food that is so named because when you eat it, it will szechuan fire.

Of the burning questions gaining our attention these days, perhaps the most vexing is the following: Why do we drive on a parkway and park on a driveway?

"Honey," called the crazy man as he opened the door to leave the house, "I'm off!"

A string wanders into a bar and slithers up to the counter and climbs onto a barstool.
The bartender glares at him and says, "Get out! We don't serve strings in this establishment."
Dejected, the string slides down and slithers out the door. Not one to lose a battle, the feisty little string goes around the corner of the building. Once out of sight, he twists himself into a series of loops. He then roughs up some of the loops and goes back into the bar.
Back on the barstool he looks the bartender squarely in the eye and orders a drink.
The bartender scowls at him and says, "I thought I told you we don't serve strings! You are a string, aren't you?"
The string replies, "I'm a frayed knot."

Then there was the butcher who backed into the meat grinder and got a little behind in his work.

Ostracized: converted into the size of an ostrich.

The visitors to the psychiatric hospital were shown how the facility maintains humane treatment and is at the leading edge in techniques for treating their patients.

"As we proceed through these different corridors," the head doctor was explaining, "you will notice that we try to separate the patients according to the level of their distress. The least incapacitated are in this wing. These patients can pretty much manage on their own."

In the next wing the doctor continued, "Here we have the patients who need some level of restraint and are generally on a cocktail of pscho-active drugs."

The discussion continued as the group moved through the various hospital wings. As the group approached the rear of the hospital they could hear screams, shouts and banging noises echoing through the corridors. The sounds were absolutely terrifying.

"What is happening down there?" one of the guests asked the doctor.

"We'll go downstairs and I will show you. But you must be very quiet," the doctor warned.

Down in the lower section the shouts, screams and banging practically shook the walls. Inside the lone cell in that wing there was a frantic man, wildly thrashing about. He was screaming, "Hold 'em! Hold 'em! Go long, you idiot! Block that hole! Look to the blind side, you nincompoop!"

"What happened to this poor man?" one of the guests asked.

"He is by far the saddest and most hopeless case we have ever known," the doctor lamented. "He was the head coach of a football team that lost 79 to 78 in the Rosebowl."

The man was driving along the superhighway, when he came upon a toll booth. The sign said, "Pay Toll, 1000 Feet Ahead."

As he passed, he handed a millipede to the booth attendant.

A man was driving his Cadillac wildly through the streets of Pompano, Spain. The town had just begun the rush of bulls toward the stadium for the big day of bullfighting.

As the man swerved recklessly around the corner, one of the bulls stepped in the way and was clobbered by the big car. The Mayor of the town awarded the driver the tail and the ears.

Brontosaurus: why Mr. Bronto knows where we are.

Two gentle elderly ladies were discussing their vacation plans for the coming year.

"Karen, where did you go last year?" the first lady asked.

"I went to Cancun, Mexico," she answered. "A most beautiful, beautiful spot. How about you?"

The first lady responded, "Well, Karen, last year I saw the world. Next year I want to go someplace else."

A hunchback wandered over to a well-dressed man standing at a bus stop.

"Buddy, can you help me?" the hunchback asked him. "I have fallen on hard times. Can you lend me ten bucks?"

The man reached into his pocket and produced a ten dollar bill and handed it to the poor soul. The hunchback took the money, thanked the man and started to walk away.

"Excuse me, Sir," the man called after the hunchback, "When are you going to pay me back?"

The hunchback answered, "When I straighten out."

The Knights of the Round Table, that most revered of legends, were called into action by Arthur, their King.

"We have been called to the highest duty," he told his forces, "and we must fight for the very honor and survival of our esteemed kingdom."

The King then turned to Sir Lancelot. "You, my most trusted of the trusted .... I am asking you to stay here in the castle and protect my most cherished wife, Guinevere, from any intruders. She has been fitted with a chastity belt and I am entrusting you with the key. I know that you will do anything to protect her very honor and sanctity."

Arthur and the remaining Knights then rode off on their quest. About three miles out from the kingdom, Arthur saw a dust cloud rising in the distance. It was a rider coming toward them at great speed.

The troops were halted allowing the rider to catch up to them. It was Sir Lancelot.

"Sire," Sir Lancelot frantically called to Arthur, "you have given me the wrong key!"

A New York City cabby was asked by a bystander, "How do I get to Carnegie Hall?"

The cabby told him, "Practice! Practice! Practice."

Picture on the wall to the vase of flowers: "I didn't do it. Honest! I was framed."

The cannibal cook was preparing his latest missionary find. He kept a careful eye on the missionary, all the while adding the proper herbs and spices.

About a half hour later the cannibal chief wandered over to see how dinner was progressing. The chief leaned over the huge pot and noticed that it was empty.

"Where did our supper go?" the chief demanded.

"Yow," the cook exclaimed when he looked into the pot, "he convinced me that a watched pot never boils."

Snowstorm to the road: "Catch my drift?"

*Now on to Adam and Eve where we can get, if not the absolutely worst, at least the absolutely oldest jokes in the world.*

Eve: "Adam, are you seeing someone else?"
Adam, looking around: "Like, who?"

Eve: "Adam, I suspect you of seeing another woman."
Adam: "You caught me. I am turning over a new leaf."

The Bible depicts the world's first baseball game. It starts out with the words "In the Big Inning...."

The minister noticed that the milk being served in the rectory was spoiling. The children in the day school needed milk and the stores were closed on Sunday.
The minister took the milk and said a prayer over it. He then served it to the children and it tasted fresh and sweet.
"That's amazing," one of the mothers declared to him. "How did you do that?"
"I Pastor-ized it," he answered.

Brontosaurus: how Mr. Bronto felt after he fell on his tush.

If some people carefully examined their family tree they would see many of their ancestors hanging from it.

"Mrs. Johnson," the voice cried out from outside, "your husband has been run over by a steamroller."
"I'm in the shower right now," she answered, "just slip him under the door."

The Cardinal played hooky one Sunday and went to the golf course.

While he played, Saint Peter cried out to God, "Look there. That Cardinal is committing, I dare say, a cardinal sin!"

God said assuredly, "I will punish him." With that He reached down and took the next ball the Cardinal hit and carried it 465 yards and deposited it for a hole-in-one.

"How is that punishing him?" Saint Peter asked.

"Whom can he tell?" God replied.

The pet store now offers all-cat fish food.

Three scientists were arguing over what the world's greatest invention has been.

"Gentlemen," the first scientist began, "I believe that you are on the right track. We must, however, consider that the wheel itself must be the greatest invention of all time. Just think of all of the devices that have derived from that so simple, yet so important machine. Where would technology be had it never been invented?"

"True, true," the second scientist chimed in, "but most probably the wheel was being invented in many places at the same time and it would have come about no matter what. I submit that the greatest invention of all time has been the laser. Just think of the medical procedures, the industrial applications, the information transmissions that have been made possible through this device. There is no doubt of its implications and importance."

The third scientist declared, "No, no, no. You are both way off the mark. The greatest invention of all time is clearly the thermos bottle."

"What? the thermos bottle?" the other two asked simultaneously.

"Let me explain," the third scientist continued. "If you take hot liquid and place it into a thermos bottle, what happens?"

The second scientist answered, "Why, it stays hot, of course."

"Correct," the third man went on. "Now what happens when in place of the hot liquid, you put a cold liquid into a thermos bottle. What happens then?"

The first man answered, "Why, it stays cold. Most definitely, it stays cold."

"Again, correct," the third scientist said. "How does it know?"

"My doctor thought I was suffering from heartburn .... Then I showed him this book; he burned it instead."

Then there was the karate expert who was drafted into the Army. The first time he saw an officer, he saluted and bashed his own brains out.

"Life stinks," declared the customer, "and I don't like Ladies Home Journal much, either."

Werewolf: a type of dog kept in a warehouse.

"How many employees work at this facility?" the visitor asked the personnel manager.
"Thirty six," the personnel manager replied.
"Only thirty six people work in a large building like this?" the visitor responded in surprise.
"Oh, right!" the manager went on. "We *employ* 1018 people here, but only thirty six work."

Then there was the dog whose nighttime performance was a howling success.

The man is awakened by a soft, rhythmic knocking on his apartment door.
"Who's there?" he called through the locked door.
"Three birds are watching. All is calm," came the reply.
"What was that?" the man asked.
"Three birds are watching. All is calm," the stranger repeated.
"I don't understand," the man said, perplexed.
"Three birds are watching. All is calm," the voice said again.
"Oh, yeah....right," the man said. "You've got the wrong room. Epstein the spy is upstairs in 303."

If your pet is a police dog, where is his badge?

Winston Churchill, the famous former Prime Minister of England, was given honorary United States citizenship. He accepted the honor very graciously.

To his surprise, within a few days he was sent a 1040 Form from the IRS. He looked at it, read the booklet, and then he declared: "Never in the course of history have so many owed so much to so few!"

Teacher in Latin class: "Can anyone tell me the derivation of the word 'auditorium?' "

Student: "It comes from 'audio, which means 'to hear' and 'taurus,' which means 'bull.'"

An elderly woman stops at the street corner and looks around to get her bearings. She spots a bearded hippie standing a few feet away and saunters over to ask him a question.

"Does the downtown trolley come this way?" she asks.

He replies: "Doo dah! Doo dah!"

The little lady went into the Chinese restaurant and took a seat near the beautiful waterfall in the middle. The waiter brought her the menu of the day.

She carefully examined all of the delicacies that the establishment had to offer and then placed her order.

After a while the waiter came over and moved the nearby tables out of the way to make room for an enormous bowl set on wheels.

"Why, that bowl is absolutely *huge*," the little lady shouted. "Why are you bringing out such a gigantic bowl?"

"Don't blame us, Lady," the waiter responded, "you're the one who ordered Won Ton soup."

Paradox: two doctors.

I am going to subscribe to Electricity Review. I only want the *current* issue.

Deep sea swordfish addressing the ocean bottom: "You are fine, upstanding and the silt of the earth."

My barber was arrested and his shop was closed down. The authorities claimed he ran a clip joint.

Colonel Sanders had done it all in the world of chickens. His food chain had spread worldwide. He then decided to branch out into law enforcement.

"Why I do believe that chickens can be trained to be outstanding enforcers of our domestic laws," he declared one day to the Board of Directors of Kentucky Fried Chicken, his famous company. And so he set out to develop a crime-fighting chicken force.

Through careful genetic development he was able to produce a special chicken that was much taller, heavier and stronger than all other chickens. In addition, his chickens had developed splines at the ends of their wings that performed very much like fingers on a hand.

After months of training, the Colonel was ready to invite his Board to observe his force at work.

"I want you all to witness my chickens in action in the field," he told his Board members. "We will all go into the inner city and watch one of my finest on duty."

The entourage departed by bus to the bowels of the most desperate part of the city. They all stayed aboard the bus for safety.

"There's one of my enforcers now," the Colonel called out. The large bird was stalking a crime in progress.

Suddenly the bird surged into action and dove directly into the middle of three robbers holding up a local citizen.

Without hesitation the plucky chicken began whapping the hoodlums unmercifully with the ends of its wings.

While the chicken was flogging one of the perpetrators into submission, a Board Member shrieked out, "Good grief! What on earth is that bird doing?"

A second Board member replied, "Why, that Kentucky Fried chicken is finger-licking hood."

The cannibal chief's son grabs a baseball and starts a game of catch with the missionary.

The chief, watching the goings on, angrily storms out of his hut and yells at his boy, "How many times have I told you not to play with your food?"

Sign in a do-it-yourself clothing store: Suit Yourself.

Sign in a do-it-yourself surgery center: Suture Self.

The little car was chugging merrily along the highways and byways when it struck a group of iron bars strewn across the road. All of the tires went flat!

A little while later another car came along and stopped to help. The second car assessed the unfortunate situation and after much thought it offered its advice.

"Looks like it's time for you to retire," it said.

The wedding guest watched with great admiration as Robert and Roberta Hall made their solemn vows before the altar.

As fate and poor conscience would have it, the two began to cheat on one another after only a few days of marriage. First he incorporated a mistress. Angered, she began to see other men.

Before long both Robert and Roberta were bringing lover after lover into the house. The wedding guest was angered to the point of distraction.

One day the guest traveled to the less-than-happy couple's house. He knocked on the door and they both ran to answer.

Upon their opening the door, the guest knocked them both unconscious with two mighty punches.

When asked why he committed such an act, he replied, "I went to deck the Halls; their vows were folly."

Post-World War III horror story: The only person left on earth is sitting in her house, when there is a knock at the door.

The leader of the revolutionary forces was captured by the Government's troops. The search for him had been long and costly and it was a grand day for the President's army.

It was indeed a sad day for the revolution, when he was tried and convicted of treason. The people filled the streets to express their sorrow.

The next day at dawn, the leader was lead to the courtyard, head proudly held high, to face the execution of his sentence. The firing squad was assembled and readied in position. The men loaded their weapons and placed them by their sides in preparation.

After the leader was tied to the post, the commander of the squad asked him if he had any last wishes.

"I would like a cigarette," he said with a firm voice.

The commander slapped him across the face and screamed, "Fool! Don't you realize that the Surgeon General has determined that cigarette smoking can be harmful to your health?"

A man had been very troubled by nightmares, so he decided to seek professional help and made an appointment with a psychologist.

The psychologist began the examination of his new patient.

"I am going to show you a series of ink blots," he explained. "These are called the Rorschach Test. I will show you an ink blot and you will tell me what comes to your mind."

The psychologist turned the pages to the first ink blot and showed the image to his patient.

"What do you see?" he asked.

"I see a naked couple making mad, passionate love."

"H-m-m-m-m. Let's try another one. Now what do you see in this ink blot?"

"I see another naked couple making mad, passionate love."

The psychologist continued through the book and each time the patient's answer was the same.

"You really have a dirty mind," the psychologist exclaimed.

"Me?" replied the patient, "*you're* the one showing me the dirty pictures."

The construction worker fell three stories into a pile of gravel. Miraculously he only suffered minor cuts and bruises and a broken hand, which his doctor set in a cast. Several weeks later the doctor examined the hand and, finding the healing successful, began to remove the cast.

"Doc, when this cast is removed, will I be able to play piano?"

"Of course you will," the doctor replied.

"You're a wonderful doctor," the worker retorted, "I never played piano before."

Upon crossing the border, the traveler saw a billboard that read "Drink Canada Dry." He tried his darndest.

My name is Cliff. Drop over anytime.

It was a tough season for the coach. The pre-season reviews said that his was the team to beat. And that is exactly what everybody did.

The airplane was cruising along at 37,000 feet. The flight up to then had been smooth and uneventful.

Suddenly the Captain announced, "All passengers please securely fasten your seat belts. We are approaching an area of unsettled weather."

Unsettled was the understatement of the year. The plane thrashed about violently, tossing packages from the overhead compartments and lurching passengers to and fro in their seats.

Scared out of her wits a gentle lady screamed out, "Please! Somebody do something religious!"

A man got up and took up a collection.

Ed: "Did you fly in all the way from Fort Lauderdale?"
Ned: "I sure did."
Ed: "Gosh! You're arms must be awfully tired."

The motorist was speeding through town, when the police car caught up with him and pulled him over.

After running a check on the license plate the policeman went over to the motorist and said, "The computer notified me that you have been caught for speeding eleven times this year. What is it going to take to stop this from happening again?"

The motorist replied, "A faster car."

Suppress a sneeze and blow your mind.

Then there was the woman who passed her baking class with flying crullers.

Bill: "I like your pants. What are they?"
Will: "Jeans."
Bill: "Then what is Jean wearing?"

A young man looking for a job went to an employment agency. After filling out the necessary forms, he was interviewed by the counselor.

Counselor: "You didn't put down your education level. How far in school did you go?"
Young Man: "I quit school after the fourth grade."
Counselor: "Why? What happened?"
Young Man: "I repeated the fourth grade six times."
Counselor: "*Six* times?"
Young Man: "Well, you see. I was a hardship case. My father was in the fifth grade. How would it have looked if I passed him?"

Then there was the milking machine that went haywire and caused udder chaos.

Camel: a horse designed by a committee.

The manager was inspecting the work place. In one room toward the rear of the plant he observed two men at work. One man was sweeping the floor and the other one was hanging from the ceiling by holding onto a large overhead hook. The manager studied the scene for a few minutes, trying to comprehend what was happening.

"What in the blazes are you doing?" he yelled to the man hanging from the ceiling.

"I'm the light," the man replied.

"The what? The light?" the manger exclaimed.

"Sure," the man continued, "this room needed a light, so I volunteered."

The manager restrained his growing anger, but he warned the man, "When I come through here again, you had better be working!" He then stormed off to continue his inspection.

Nearly four hours passed and the manager decided to revisit that room.

Upon entering the room he saw the man still hanging from the ceiling, while the other man was sweeping the floor.

"All right!" the manager screamed, "I warned you. You're fired! Clear out of here!"

The first man dropped down from the hook, gathered his belongings and left. The man sweeping then put down the broom and began to leave, also.

"Where do you think *you're* going?" the manager yelled to the second man.

The second man looked back at the manager, "I'm not going to work with no light!"

The boss went to his employee's house for dinner. The worker had hoped to impress the Old Stuffed Shirt and maybe position himself for a nice raise.

Halfway through the dinner, the worker's little five-year old daughter wandered over to the boss and began to stare at him.

"Why are you staring at me like that?" the boss gently asked the little tike.

She replied, "I can't see what my Daddy means. He said you have two faces."

Helen: "What's green and white, has nine legs, four pinchers and goes r-r-r-r-a-a-a-r-r-r-r?"

Ellen: "I give up. What?"

Helen: "I don't know, but it's crawling up your pants leg."

The old man had no teeth for the past twenty years. Finally, he went to a dentist to get fitted with false teeth.

After the job was completed, the dentist asked him, "Well, how do you like them?"

The old man replied, "Looks like the next time something comes up, I'll finally be able to put the bite on."

Then there was the Marine lieutenant who mistreated his men. He was court-martialed because he was rotten to the Corps.

Then there was the statistician who drowned in a river of average depth three feet.

A man was walking through the woods, when a raccoon charged out and bit him on the leg. Frightened, he rushed immediately to his doctor.

The doctor examined him and drew the normal body fluids for lab testing.

A few days later the doctor called the man into his office and told him the bad news. "I'm sorry, Mr. Timkins, but you have rabies."

The man grabbed a piece of paper and began to write frantically.

The doctor put his hand on the man's shoulder and said, "You don't have to write your will and testament. Rabies is curable and I believe we caught it in time."

"What will and testament?" the man shot back, "I'm making a list of people I am going to bite."

What do you get when you pour boiling water down a rabbit hole? Hot, cross bunnies.

The restaurant owner decided to expand his product offering, so he started a drive-through custard business. People could order any type of custard known.

At first the business thrived. As time went on, however, business dropped off dramatically and the stands were closed one-by-one until only one outlet remained.

The restaurant owner decided to name it "Custard's Last Stand."

A store owner was bitten by a radioactive fly. Within a few weeks he turned into the insect himself. The transformation forced him to only be able to work after sundown. So he opened a fly-by-night business.

An actor was bitten by a radioactive fly. Within a few weeks his transformation to a fly was complete.

Unfortunately, his career was reduced to only parts in horror movies, and only those requiring large insects.

"Doesn't what happened bother you?" a press agent asked him one day.

"Well, you know what they say," he replied. "That's show biz-z-z-z-z-z-z-z."

Paranoid: two noids [nerds] from Brooklyn.

A man drove into town to do some shopping. A few hours later he went to his car to unload his purchases. He was horror struck to see smoke pouring out from under the vehicle.

"Great Scott," he cried out, "what could be wrong!"

He opened the hood and pulled off the carburetor cap. He then removed the valve cover. He used all of his meager knowledge of cars. Having still not found the problem he began to frantically ask passersby for help.

Many people quickly moved away from the smoking vehicle, but a few Good Samaritans did stop to help. Soon there were about 10 people milling around the car.

The smoke continued to pour forth while the rest of the engine was disassembled piece-by-piece. Next the exhaust system was dismantled.

Five hours had passed and nobody could understand why the car still billowed out smoke. Meanwhile, the man collected the hundreds of parts that had been strewn around the car.

Finally a service truck on its way to answer an emergency pulled over. The man in the truck got out, went over to the car and looked the situation over. He examined the collection of parts on the ground and looked at the car.

"What's the problem?" the first man asked.

The service man replied, "You're parked over a steam grate."


A man went on a long vacation trip to the South Pacific. He asked his brother to watch his prized parrot in his absence.

A few days later he called his brother to ask how things were going and his brother replied, "Oh, your parrot is dead."

"What!" screamed the man. "My $3,000 bird is dead!"

The man took a minute to compose himself and then explained to his brother, "You know how attached I was to that bird. You could have gently broken the news to me."

"For instance," he continued, "you could have said that Polly had escaped from her cage and landed on the roof. I would have been concerned, but still hopeful. The next day I would have called and you could have told me that Polly tried to fly, but caught her foot on a shingle in a freak accident and fell to the ground.

"You would have explained that she was badly hurt but was under the care of the Veterinarian. The next day you could have told me that Polly took a turn for the worst, but the doctor was still hopeful.

"Finally, when I called the day after that, you could have broken the bad news that Polly had died despite the best medical treatment. I would have been saddened, but at least I would have been prepared for the news."

The man calmed himself down and then slowly asked his brother, "Anyway, how's Mom?"

"She's on the roof," the brother replied.

Fred: "What are you doing, Ned?"
Ned: "I'm writing a great book of fiction."
Fred: "That's a novel idea."

Teacher: "What is capital punishment?"
Student: "Listening to a speech by your congressman."

The little elderly lady was busy knitting socks, when her best friend came over for a visit.

"So what are you doing, Maude?" the friend asked.

"I'm knitting socks for my nephew, Henry. He's off at college now," the little lady replied.

"Why are you knitting three socks?" the friend questioned.

"Because," the little lady answered, "his mother told me he had grown another foot, since I last saw him."

Boycott: a boy scout's bed.

Punishment: the art of making puns.

The rich man needed surgery, so the doctor performed a total cashectomy.

The couple at the next table in the restaurant did nothing but complain and complain. First, the food was too hot. Then the food was too cold. Next the coffee was weak. The meat was too tough. "What is the problem with those people?" the poor hapless man at the first table asked the waiter.

"They are whining and dining," the waiter replied.

The young cowboy was out on his first trail ride. Being new and inexperienced, he was given all of the chores nobody else wanted.

"You can now make us coffee," the trail boss ordered him. "Tell us when it's done."

The young cowboy went to work and about 30 minutes later called out, "Coffee is ready."

The other cowboys gathered around as he poured the elixir into their cups.

"This is the best coffee we've ever had," the trail boss said, "how did know how to make it?"

The young cowboy replied, "I just boiled mud until I could stand up a horseshoe in it."

Teetotaler: the man responsible for counting how much tea is served.

The father asked his little son, "How did your sandlot baseball game go today?"

The boy replied, "I hit a run home."

"You mean a home run," the father corrected him.

"No," the boy answered, "I mean a run home. I hit the ball through Mr. Thompkin's window."

The quarterback was sad because his girlfriend was true to the end.

Joe: "What did cavemen do on Saturday night."
Moe: "They went out night clubbing."

The doctor examining the patient kept coming back to the patient's belly button.
"You weren't in the Army, were you?" the patient asked.
"Why, no," the doctor responded.
"I didn't think so," added the patient, "you seem like a navel man."

The avid golfer was readying his ball at the fifteenth hole, when he noticed a huge flash and a mushroom cloud rising in the distance. He stood there for a moment in stunned silence.
"Good, God!" he screamed to his friend. "That's an A-bomb blast! World War III has started!"
"Go ahead and tee off," his friend said calmly, "the shock wave won't get here for at least ten minutes."

Ned: "Why don't you like golfers?"
Ed: "They are always getting teed off."

Sign on golf course: Par 4, Next Rough.

Astronaut to space center: "Do you suppose that we will find any life on Mars?"
Space Center: "Only if you land there on Saturday night."

Seafood diet: an eating regimen in which you rush out and eat everything you see.

*Nursery rhymes, those not-so-innocent manifestations of childhood, should not be immune from jabs, so here goes.*

The local news crews were alerted to a riot in progress at the State Penitentiary. The inmates were uprising against what they felt was poor food quality.

When the crews arrived, they were greeted by a large crowd of prisoners gathered in the prison exercise yard. The crowd was chanting, "Peas porridge hot. Peas porridge cold. Peas porridge in the pot, nine days old."

Jack and Jill went up the hill
To fetch a pail of water.
Jack fell down and broke his crown
And Jill sued the County for negligence.

Baa, baa black sheep
Have you any wool?
"Whattaya think? I'm polyester?"

Jack and Jill went up the hill
To fetch a pail of water.
Jack fell down and broke his crown
And was denied insurance due to self-inflicted injury.

Jack be nimble.
Jack be quick.
Jack makes a dollar an hour
And forty dollars a wick.

Old Mother Hubbard went to her cupboard
To fetch her poor dog a bone.
When she got there, the cupboard was bare,
So the dog took one out of her leg.

Little Miss Muffett,
Sat on a tuffett,
Eating of curds and whey.
Along came a large spider
That sat down beside her
And asked, "What's a tuffett?"

There was an old woman
Who lived in a shoe.
She had so many children
The IRS didn't know what to do.

*And speaking of vampires...Hey, I had to change the subject somehow!*

The vampires in Transylvania love baseball. They use bats and they all have a ball.

Count Dracula finally realized his boyhood dream to participate in Major League baseball. He was selected to be the first base vampire.

Werewolf: "I don't understand your getting married. You! The great Count Dracula! What did you ever see in her?"
Count Dracula: "She was a vamp."

Then there was the vampire who was awarded a law degree without even having attended school. He was already a bloodsucker.

The lawyer was a real ambulance chaser. He spent his free time scouting hospital emergency rooms for potential clients.
One day he was sizing up the candidates in a crowded local emergency room, when he spotted a battered looking patient swathed

in bandages, sitting alone in the corner. The lawyer went over to the man and delivered his pitch.

"We can certainly sue the motorist that hit you," the lawyer began. "We have to take these careless, unthinking drivers off the road."

"There was no other motorist," the patient replied, "I was alone on the road when my car went out of control."

"We can subrogate against the car manufacturer," the lawyer continued, "they have no business allowing such defective and dangerous vehicles on the road."

"Oh, not at all," the man responded, "it was a wonderful car and in top condition when the accident occurred."

"No doubt the State was at fault due to poor road surface maintenance."

"Certainly not. The road was in perfect condition, having been recently repaved."

"The guard rails should have held you back on any curve and prevented the accident." The lawyer was becoming exasperated.

"The road was perfectly straight with wide, smooth shoulders and the trees were more than fifty feet back. There was no need for a guard rail and none was present."

"The State should take responsibility for not posting the proper signs warning of the dangers of inclement weather."

"The weather was absolutely beautiful and the sun was behind me the whole time."

"It's people like you," the lawyer snapped, "that give the legal profession a bad name."

The college football coach watched his men at practice. First one fumbled, then another one dropped an easy pass. The line .... oh, the line! The defense looked like the Keystone Cops meet the gridiron.

"You Bozos," screamed the coach, "Why, my grandmother

shows more experience than you guys!"

"That's unfair, Coach," the defensive guard complained, "she's older."

The little ant was running at a great rate of speed along the edge of the cereal box.

"What are you doing?" another ant asked.

"I'm following instructions," he replied. "I'm tearing along the dotted line."

The IRS wished me a Happy Birthday and many happy returns.

The man was horrified to learn that he was going to be audited by the IRS. He scurried around the house and his office, scrounging up every bit of evidence and information he could find.

The fateful day arrived and the poor, hapless soul cowered in the shadow of the IRS building. The huge structure seemed so cold and foreboding.

He slowly entered the monstrous lobby and went to the fiftieth floor, passed through five massive sets of double doors and settled into what seemed like an electric chair in the waiting room.

After an hour, his name was called. He slowly and nervously entered the auditor's office.

"Please take a chair," the auditor said.

"Oh, thank you," the man said relieved. "Can I make one request?"

"Certainly," the auditor responded.

"Can you help me get it into the trunk of my car?" the man asked.

Joe: "How did your interview with the IRS. go?"
Jim: "Fine. I was hired, but I turned them down."
Joe: "Why?"
Jim: "I was told it would be a taxing job."

Ben: "I got a haircut today."
Glen: "Why didn't you get them *all* cut?"

The kindly old lady opened the door to her refrigerator and to her surprise there was a little bunny rabbit sleeping inside.

"Oh, my word," the old lady said with surprise, "what in the world are you doing in there?"

"This is a Westinghouse, isn't it?" the bunny asked.

"Why, yes," she replied.

"Well, I'm westing," he said.

Joe: "How was your first day as an elevator operator?"
Jim: "It had its ups and downs."

Sign inside an elevator: "'9' button out of order. Please press '5' and '4.'"

The king looked out over his land from the top of his castle.

"This land seems so barren at times," he said to his duke, "there is certainly something missing, but I do not know what it is."

"I know what it might be," the duke responded. "There just are no birds in any great number; so their songs cannot be heard. More birds would certainly help cheer the kingdom up."

After considering the idea, the king concluded that the duke was indeed correct and he called a meeting of his trusted innermost cabinet.

The cabinet members studied and rejected many proposals on

the best way to increase the bird population. Finally, one member rose and declared, "Gentlemen, I have the solution. We will increase the stock of fish in the Royal Lake by diverting the nearby river. In this way, we will attract more fish-eating birds."

The idea was accepted and work was immediately started on the project. After four months, the river connection was completed and the fish spawning began in the Royal Lake.

Within a few months terns arrived, drawn by the opulence of fish. As time passed, more and more terns flocked to the kingdom. The king and all of his subjects rejoiced at the merry squealing coming from the birds.

Alas, too much of a good thing proved itself not to be welcome and the birds soon became a nuisance. The king ordered his cabinet to find a way to rid the kingdom of this new menace the huge population of birds had created.

Horns were played day and night by the Royal Trumpeters, but the bird population still increased.

Firecrackers and fireworks were exploded to scare off the birds, but still no success was gained against their increasing population.

After several more frustrating attempts to drive the birds off, the king decided that the only course of action was to destroy them. Sadly, and with great reservation, he ordered the Royal Knights to arm themselves with slings and stones. They were to then fan out through the kingdom, firing on the birds wherever they were found.

The king declared, "You, my most trusted legion, will scour the corners and crevices of the entire kingdom. You will seek out every single bird."

Looking squarely at the Knights aligned before him, he said, "You must not leave a single tern unstoned."

The peasant couple brought their infant child to see the queen. During the visit the child wet its diaper and the queen changed the subject.

Doctor: "I'm afraid you are pregnant."
Young woman: "*You're* afraid? Wait until I tell my *boyfriend*."

Larry: "I haven't seen Bob lately. How's he doing in his new job at the paper mill?"
Gary: "Oh, didn't you hear? He had a terrible accident. He fell into a paper towel machine."
Larry: "How did it turn out?"
Gary: "He's on a roll."

Okinawa: how fast the woodcutter can cut down oak trees.

A man landed a job with a construction crew. His duty was to supply the bricks and mortar.

He found the job fascinating and he learned much about bricks and mortar. He even started a brick collection. As the variety of the building projects increased, so did the variety in his brick collection.

Soon his garage was so full of bricks that he could no longer put the car inside. He could now not help himself and he collected more and more bricks.

He refused to allow his precious bricks to be left out in the elements, so when his garage was full, he began to store the bricks in the basement.

At first his wife tolerated his eccentricity, but when the bricks were brought into the house itself, she put her foot down.

"You have to seek professional help," she beseeched him, "this brick fetish of yours is starting to ruin our marriage."

He refused to accept that he had a problem and he collected

more and more bricks.

Finally, his wife left him and eventually his boss fired him. Soon, thereafter, he lost his house and car. Destitute and downtrodden, he had no place to go.

One day while sleeping in the street, he heard church bells in the distance. Remembering that he was born a Catholic, he sought out the church.

Inside the church he went to the Rectory and asked the priest for help. He explained the whole situation of his life and how he came to his present state of affairs.

"You say you were born a Catholic," the priest said.

"Yes, Father, but I have not stepped inside a church in over thirty years," the man answered.

"Tell me," the priest went on, thinking about this man's state of affairs, "do you know how to make a novena?"

"Father," the man said, brightening up, "if you've got the plans, I've got the bricks."

Rock and Roll: comparison between sandwich bread in a school cafeteria and sandwich bread at home.

It's not that I'm afraid to die. I just don't want to be there when it happens.

Stampede: the postage stamp used to mail a centipede.

A friend is someone who will help you move. A real friend is someone who will help you move a body.

Chow Mein: the hair on the back of the head of a Chinese dog.

Subgum: the material that holds a submarine together.

Person answering the phone: "Hello?"
Caller: "Is Sal there?"
Person: "You've got the wrong number."
Caller: "If I dialed the wrong number, why did you answer?"

A little boy opened a lemonade stand in front of his house. A few minutes later a gentleman in a business suit stopped at the stand.
"How much is a glass of your lemonade?" the man asked.
"Twenty five cents," the little boy responded.
The man drank the lemonade. "My, that is delicious. I'll have another one."
"That'll be five dollars up front," the little boy demanded.
"Five dollars!" the man exclaimed. "Why so much more for a second glass?"
"It contains the antidote," the little boy answered.

The revolutionary leader was asked if he had any last statement before the firing squad was ordered to shoot.
"I regret that I have but one life to give for my country!" the leader said.
The squad leader added, "So do I."

Hal: "On a scale of one-to-ten, how would you rate me as a friend?"
Al: "Oh, you are definitely a 'ten' "
Hal: "Hey, thank you."
Al: "U-h-h, let's make that a 'one.' "

Barroom: a room where lawyers meet.

Barroom: the sound a cannon makes.

Barroom: how a drunk refers to the bathroom.

A dog trots into a bar, takes his place on the barstool and orders a whiskey.

"That'll be twenty dollars," the bartender tells the dog, counting on the pooch's naivety.

The canine reaches into his fur and pulls out a twenty dollar bill and paws it over to the bartender.

"You know," the bartender says, trying to make small talk, "we don't get many dogs in here."

"No wonder! At twenty dollars a drink!" the dog exclaims.

A dog trots into a bar, takes his place on the barstool and orders a whiskey.

"We don't serve dogs here," the bartender tells him.

"That's fine with me," the dog responds, "I'm not hungry. I only want a drink."

An elderly businessman arrives in town for one evening for the big trade convention. At the hotel he discovers that his room has been rented to someone else. He raises a big fuss and finally wins a major concession from the hotel reservation staff.

"We'll give you the bridal suite," the manager concedes, "but you must be out first thing in the morning. That suite has been rented to a young and *very* wealthy couple who will be arriving early."

The elderly man accepts and discovers that his room is very well equipped and he has a wonderful evening in the plush suite.

Early the next morning, as promised, he gathers his belongings and leaves the hotel.

About an hour later he discovers that he has left his umbrella in the room. Upon arriving back at the hotel he heads directly to the bridal suite. As he is about to try the door he hears a couple's voices coming from inside the room..

"Ah, this hair; so beautiful and it is all mine," a male voice says lovingly. "Ah, these eyes; so beautiful, and they are all mine. Ah, these lips; so lush and full, and they are all mine. Ah ...."

"When you get to the umbrella," the elderly man shouts, "its mine!"

Umbrella Policy: insurance for when your umbrella is injured.

The troubled man seeks out psychiatric help. He follows up on the referral from a friend and makes an appointment with a well-known doctor in town.

The doctor's aid takes down all the preliminary information and brings the man into the doctor's office, where he assumes the traditional position on the couch.

The man tells the doctor his entire life story, one-hour-at-a-time, for several years. All through each session the doctor remains stone silent as the man speaks. There isn't even an acknowledgment as the man leaves after each one-hour session has ended.

One day the man demands that the doctor explain to him what he has found out to date and what his recommendations are.

The doctor turns slowly to the man, looks at him and with a much surprised expression and exclaims, "Who are *you*?"

Bill: "Doesn't our National Anthem have a part about famous composers."

Gill: "Which part?"

Bill: "The one that goes '.... and the rockets' red glare, the Brahms, Bernstein in air ....'"

The price you pay for playing the music of Franz Liszt: the Liszt price.

The judge begrudgingly accepts the psychiatric panel's decision that the defendant be ruled legally insane.

"You're no more insane than I am," the judge snorted at the defendant as the trial resumed.

"Well, Your Honor," the defendant retorted, "maybe my lawyer can get you off, too."

April 16: the day of National Relief.

Taxes: the very large state below Oklahoma.

Jeff: "I'm not going to pay my taxes until Halloween."
Jethro: "Why on Earth would you choose that date?"
Jeff: "In that way I might have a ghost of a chance of not going to jail."

IRS. auditor: "It says here that you gave $29,500.00 to charities last year."
The auditee: "What's wrong with that?"
IRS. Auditor: "Well, you only made $26,973.35."
The auditee: "Hey, I'm a soft touch."

Catalog: a listing of the cattle you own.

First Farmer: "I'm pretty successful; I get forty gallons of milk a day from my herd."
Second Farmer: "Heck, that's nothing. I get sixty two gallons a day from mine."
First Farmer: "How's that possible? We have the same number of cows."
Second Farmer: "I use pliers."

Horoscope: your mirror after forty.

Jim: "I try to do a good job. I really do try."
Tim: "I see that. You are the most trying person I know."

Dandruff: a little boy saying Dan plays rough.

Advertisement for a Drivers Education School: "In a hurry to learn to drive? We offer a crash course."

"Thought I went home, didn't you? Well, home is where the heart is .... or in this case, where the heart*burn* is!"

At the piano recital the handsome, dashing pianist stepped out onto the stage. The women swooned with passion as he flipped back his long, flowing hair.

"He's *so-o-o-o* unbelievably incredible," a woman up front purred to her friend.

"You don't know him like I do," her friend snapped, "He's a real pig. The way he looks at women and the way he sneers at them."

"But," the woman retorted "he only plays the music of Chopin."

"What's the significance of that?" her friend asked.

"I guess that makes him a male, Chopinesque pig," the woman responded.

The young, pert coed went to college to get her MRS.

The young boy from Mexico was given a rare opportunity. His parents managed to save enough money to send him to the United States for a two-week visit with a friend living in New York City.

During his visit, the friend and his family took him to Yankee Stadium to watch a double-header with the Detroit Lions.

When the two weeks were up, the young boy bid a tearful farewell to his wonderful friend and returned home.

"How was your visit to New York City?" his Mother and Father asked almost simultaneously.

The young boy animatedly described all of the wonderful sights that he had seen and all of the wonderful things he had done.

"But most of all," he continued, "was how all of the people in Yankee Stadium greeted me. Yes, thousands and thousands of people greeting only me."

"What do you mean?" his Mother asked.

"When I was in the stadium, I was too small to see over the heads of everybody, so my friend helped me to climb over the back railing and stand on the stadium supports."

"And you saw everything?" his Father asked.

"Not then," the boy continued, "but soon people were handing me over each others heads until I got to the flagpole. I then climbed up the flagpole and got a most wonderful view."

"Then what happened?" his little sister asked.

"Suddenly, music began to play," he said excitedly, "and everybody in the entire stadium turned to look at me and they sang 'Jose can you see ....?' "

Propaganda: What's good for the proper goose is good for the propaganda.

Then there was the circus tumbler who one day flipped out.

Traffic was backing up at an intersection. It seemed that nobody was moving anywhere.

Finally, one frustrated driver got out of his car to find out what was causing this horrendous tie-up. He walked passed at least seventy five cars before arriving at the car responsible for the mess. He was stopped at a stop sign.

"What are you just sitting here for!" he screamed at the driver.

"I'm waiting for that sign to turn green," the driver replied.

Hangover: what your belly does after Thanksgiving dinner.

Title of the headhunters' manual: "How to Get Ahead"

Lament of the lovesick sheep: "I only think of ewe."

The Government was under fire to improve its productivity and its image. An efficiency expert was hired to study the workplace. He was then to make the proper recommendations for improvement of the overall operations.

"What do you do?" the expert asked the first man he came to.

"I do absolutely nothing. I have *never* done anything. I have been working here for twenty years and to date I have had to accomplish not one single thing," the man answered.

The expert wrote notes and then went to the next man.

"What do you do?" the expert asked the second man.

"I do absolutely nothing. I have *never* done anything. I have been working here for thirty years and to date I have had to accomplish not one single thing," the man answered.

"H-m-m-m," the expert thought, "duplication."

A man walking along a deserted downtown street spots another man banging his shoulder against the side wall of the local bank.

Stopping to watch, the man is amazed at the persistence of the other individual. Time and again he would step back ten or twelve feet, lurch forward, run toward the building and slam his shoulder against the side wall.

First Man: "Hey, Buddy! What the heck are you doing?"
Second Man: "I'm knocking over this bank."

Cantaloupe: a fruit you give to your daughter to prevent her from running away and getting married.

Fred: "What did you study in your mechanics course at college last year?"
Ed: "Oh, you know. Stress vectors, bridge forces, cantilevers."
Fred: "You mean...."
Ed: "Right. We'll have these *moments* to remember."

I was at a spaghetti dinner last week. There were several servers who kept getting in each other's' way. First they pushed and shoved, then the spaghetti itself got into the fight. Next the bowls and finally the serving instruments became embroiled in the ruckus.

Before long the servers were at each other in a full out battle. You might say it precipitated into a Tong War.

The stock market suffered a sharp loss, yesterday. Over one thousand cows died.

When is a door not a door? When it is ajar.

One day the heavyweight, middleweight and welterweight contenders all went on strike, protesting their treatment at the hands of their fight promoters.

"Gads," the commissioner complained, "it looks like we are faced with the Boxer Rebellion." *[Review your World History, folks!]*

Beaver husband to beaver wife on her birthday: "Frankly, Charlotte, I give a dam."

A little boy at Sunday church listened intently to the sermon. After the service he pulled away from his mother and ran over to the minister.

"Pastor," he called out excitedly, "is it really true that from dust we come to dust we return?"

"Well, I would express it a little differently, but in a word, yes," the minister responded.

"So that's what my mother means," the boy said with a frown.

"What does you mother say?" the minister asked.

The boy responded, "Every time she comes into my room, she looks under my bed and wonders if somebody is coming or going."

It was a tough day for the suburban police precinct. Another murder had been committed. The crime was similar to a few that had recently occurred in the city itself.

Alarm was beginning to spread throughout the area as the residents voiced their concern over the unsolved murders. To head off public outcry, the police chief formed a task force to tackle the problems and solve the crimes once and for all.

"It looks like the city crime is rapidly moving our way," the captain complained to his detective.

"I am afraid so," the detective said dejectedly, "and the pattern is repeating."

"What are the markings of the latest crime?" asked the captain.

"Well, the victim apparently had been fed a severe overdose of Cheerios. The feeding had continued until the victim expired," the detective replied.

"Cheerios, eh. Very bizarre; very bizarre indeed," the captain reflected. "what did we find last week?"

"Rice Krispies was the weapon of choice in the Third Avenue crime," the detective said. "There were two victims there. One had been fed enough Rice Krispies to choke two horses. She died. Her male companion survived, but he can't go near a grocery store now without breaking out in a sweat."

"Cheerios....Rice Krispies....Any other weapons we know of?" the captain pursued.

"Well," the detective continued, "if we go back two months we come to the first such incidence. There was a vagrant living in one of the subway stop entrances. At first we thought he had bloated from drink, but the coroner's examination revealed that he had been filled with oat meal. Stuffed like a turkey."

"What can we make out of all this?" the captain asked.

The detective responded, "I'm afraid we have a cereal killer on our hands."

Mechanics lesson: the sum of torque equals conversation.

"These allegations have gotten my anger," screamed the defense lawyer. "These allegations against my client are totally unfounded"

"I submit, Your Honor," he continued, "that if you look hard at the accusations, you will find that my client is the allegatee and the prosecution's witness is the allegator."

"Help me load this television set into the back of the van," the father said to his teenage son as they were leaving the motel.

"We can't take the TV," the son exclaimed.

"We sure can," the father retorted, "that sign out front says 'Free TV,' doesn't it?"

Then there was the blood corpuscle that died in vein.

"Have a nice day," the grocery store checkout clerk wished the customer as the customer was leaving.

"Don't tell me what to do!" the customer snapped back.

At the New Jersey beach the young man on-the-make spotted a lithesome lass sunning herself on a blanket by herself. She was a vision of great beauty and he stood spellbound for several minutes. Finally, he approached her and tried to start a conversation.

"Wow. you're tanned from the sun," he commented.

"No, I'm Ashley from Newark," she replied.

The artist finished his painting, secured the hook in back and placed it prominently on the wall,

"What's that?" a passerby asked.

The artist replied, "One of my hangups."

"I'm *b-a-a-a-a-a-c-k*! Speaking of bad luck .... imagine being pressed in the pages of *this* book!"

    A superstitious man staying at a hotel began receiving a slew of omens one day. At exactly eight in the morning his breakfast came and it cost $8.00.

    He noticed that it took him eight minutes to drive to his destination as he passed eight lights – all green. During the work day he had eight meetings and each meeting had eight people including himself.

    After work ended he and seven other friends [eight again!] went to Restaurant Eight at 888 Eighth Street. His meal cost $88.88.

    "Incredible," he thought. "This is the most amazing day of my life. I must go to the race track tonight and see who's running."

At the track he studied the program and sure enough, in the eighth race Eight Ball was running.

"This is just too good to be true," he said out loud to himself.

He ran over to the window and placed $888 on Eight Ball in the eighth race.

And the horse came in eighth.

To make a long story short, don't tell it.

Sign of octopus royalty: a coat of arms.

A bit actor – or at least *he* thought of himself as an actor – was offered a bit part in a play.

"Now, don't screw this up," the director said to him. "This part is so small and so easy that I'm not even going to rehearse you. At my signal you will run out on stage and yell, 'Hark! I hear the cannon!' You got that?"

"Sure! Sure!" the actor replied excitedly and he went home a truly happy man.

All that night he kept saying to himself, "Hark! I hear the cannon! Hark! I hear the cannon!" While he showered he said, "Hark! I hear the cannon! Hark! I hear the cannon!" over and over again.

All night he dreamed that he was dashing out on the stage and yelling, "Hark! I hear the cannon! Hark! I hear the cannon!"

For the next two weeks he repeated the line at every opportunity he could. When he bought groceries, the checkout girl said, "That'll be fifteen dollars, Sir." He looked at her and shouted, "Hark! I hear the cannon!"

On the subway he was nearly arrested for creating a disturbance. "I'm releasing you in your own recognizance," the police chief told him. As he was leaving the station, he spun around, thrust his arm forward and hollered, "Hark! I hear the cannon! Hark! I hear the cannon!"

It seemed to be an eternity before the play was to open the following night. Finally, backstage he dressed in his soldier outfit and waited impatiently for the director's signal. Suddenly, the director gave the fateful gesture; the actor ran out on stage.

B-O-O-O-M!

"What the heck was that!" he shouted.

Locomotive: a crazy reason for committing a crime.

Lil: "Why are you smiling so broadly?"

Jill: "I found a fortuneteller with a really positive attitude. She just laughs so freely it just rubs off on me. I'm really very pleased with her and how she's changed my life."

Lil: "So you now have stability in your life?"

Jill: "Yup. I finally found a happy medium."

What is black and white and read all over? A newspaper.

Tim: "Why did the moron throw the clock out the window?"

Jim: "How should I know? I'm not a moron."

Harry: "I just recently attended a meeting of the Society of Movie Theater Projectionists."

Joel: "Oh, I see. A focus group."

The killer broke into the house and rounded the people up.

"Who knows where the money is?" he demanded.

He glared at each person in the room. One man squeaked out his response, "Maybe Sal over there in the corner knows."

"OK, "the killer said, "I'll go ax him."

The young man at the party began to place strips of masking tape on the host's daughter. He placed strips on her sleeves, pants legs, back of her blouse.

"Why are you doing this?" the host demanded.

"Well, your wife told me," he responded, "that your daughter has a very beautiful voice and when I go to the party tonight, I should tape her."

At the banquet the table settings were being arranged by the restaurant staff.

A not-too-bright employee left the room and returned carrying three chairs.

"Why did you bring those out?" the supervisor asked him.

"This is the O'Leary banquet, isn't it?" the employee asked.

"So?" replied the supervisor.

"Well," the employee responded, "here's three chairs for the Irish."

At the banquet, the help became a little too enthusiastic.

One young man was told to be certain that there was enough seating to accommodate all the expected guests.

He began moving the chairs from the storage room to the banquet hall.

First he brought four chairs out at one time and set them in place next to one table.

He then brought four more chairs from the storage room and placed them alongside another table.

He continued bringing chairs out until there were clearly far more chairs in the room than the table arrangement could possibly fit. But he kept on bringing out more chairs.

"What are you doing?" the supervisor yelled at him.

"I'm chair leading," the young man said.

If the Bolshevik fighters were called *Cossacks,* were the Turkish fighters under the Ottoman Empire called *Hassocks?*

Star Receiver: "Coach, I want to quit the team."
Coach: Why? You're the team star and our whole game revolves around you."
Star Receiver: "The quarterback keeps making passes at me."

Two men were talking about accidents around the workplace.
"My uncle worked for a lumber mill," the first man said, "and one day he had a horrible accident."
"What happened, if I dare ask?" the second man inquired.
The first man went on, "He was standing a little too close to the log hauler and a branch stub caught his shirt and pulled him through the saw. It cut his left side completely away."
"How utterly hideous," the second man cried. After getting his composure he asked, "How is he today?"
The first man said, "He's all right."

Al: "Where is your sister?"
Cal: "She's on the phone."
Al: "That must be quite a sight."

John: "Is that a new girlfriend I saw you with yesterday?"
Joe: "She sure is."
John: "That's her name?
Joe: "Wendy."
John: "All I want is her name. I'm not interested in a weather report."

She was the horseman's daughter and all the horse manure.

A quiet man drove his old, but reliable car to the paint shop.

"I want a new design put on my car," he told the owner.

"What kind of design?" the owner asked.

"I want S's painted all over the entire car. I would like small S's on the trunk and hood and very large S's over the sides. On the roof you should intersperse the large and small ones," the man told him.

"Let me get this straight," the owner inquired, "you want the letter 'S' painted all over your car? Nothing else? No chrome? No body color change? Just S's?"

"Yes," the man replied emphatically, "All I want are S's painted on every surface of my car."

"Any color preference or any pattern preference?"

"No, you choose the color and place them any way you want to, within the guidelines that I gave you."

The paint shop went to work placing the "S" pattern on the quiet man's car. It was an interesting job for the shop and the workers all took turns at painting the various S's. In this way a truly random pattern was obtained.

After two weeks the artwork was done and the owner called the quiet man to tell him that the car was ready.

"Beautiful! Simply beautiful!" the quiet man not-so-quietly exclaimed when he saw the masterpiece. The pattern of S's flowing gracefully over the car's surface was just as he had imagined.

"Tell me," the owner asked curiously, "why did you want this design?"

"Well, you see," the quiet man said, now quietly, "all my life people have complained that I drive so-o-o-o slowly. They would say I drive as slow as a snail. Now when they see me, they will shout, 'Look at that escargot'"

My Father's name was Ferdinand,
My Mother's name was Liza.
That is why the day I was born,
They called me Fertilizer.

The young man had always wanted to jump with a parachute. When he reached legal age he entered the Army and then joined the Paratroops.

One day he was sneezing and wheezing terribly.

"You sure sound sick," his commander commented.

"Yeah, I must have come down with something," he said.

Husband: "Don't you point your finger at me."
Wife: "Why not"
Husband: "It has a nail."

When he was born, he came out nose first. You can call him a postnasal drip.

Boyfriend: "Your daughter, Sir, is absolutely beautiful. She is wonderful. In a word, she is priceless."

Father: "I see you took her shopping already."

The wedding was a gala affair and guests came from far and wide. Everything was the best. And the food was simply wonderful, truly exceptional in every way.

A smartly dressed man was partaking of every type of food in the setting. He went back for seconds, and then for thirds. As he was heading for a fourth helping the father of the bride struck up a conversation with him.

"I don't recognize you, young man," the father queried him, "are you a friend of the groom?"

"No, not at all," he responded, "I don't know anybody on the groom's side."

"Well, then, even though I don't seem to know you," the father went on, you clearly are associated with my daughter's side of the party."

"Again, no," the young man replied, "I don't know anybody on that side either."

"Well, who do you know that brings you to this wedding?" the father asked.

"The caterer," the young man said.

Hal: "Your new girlfriend sure has a dynamite figure."
Ray: "You can say that again. Every time I touch her, she blows up."

Mother: "My son is in love."
Neighbor: "Oh, really? I thought you said he was in Jersey City."

What has four wheels and flies? A garbage truck.

The Army troops went on an overnight hike. Arriving at their destination, the soldiers pitched their tents and set up housekeeping for the evening in a clearing just out of a wooded area.

One new Private was asked to fetch firewood. He went into the woods, but could find only small kindling pieces. He then went deeper and deeper into the woods, finding larger branches as he went on.

Suddenly he realized that he didn't know his way back. In the morning the trail should become clearer to him, he thought, and so he gathered up some leaves and twigs and made a makeshift shelter for himself.

"I'm not lost," he said to himself, "I'm here. My tent is lost."

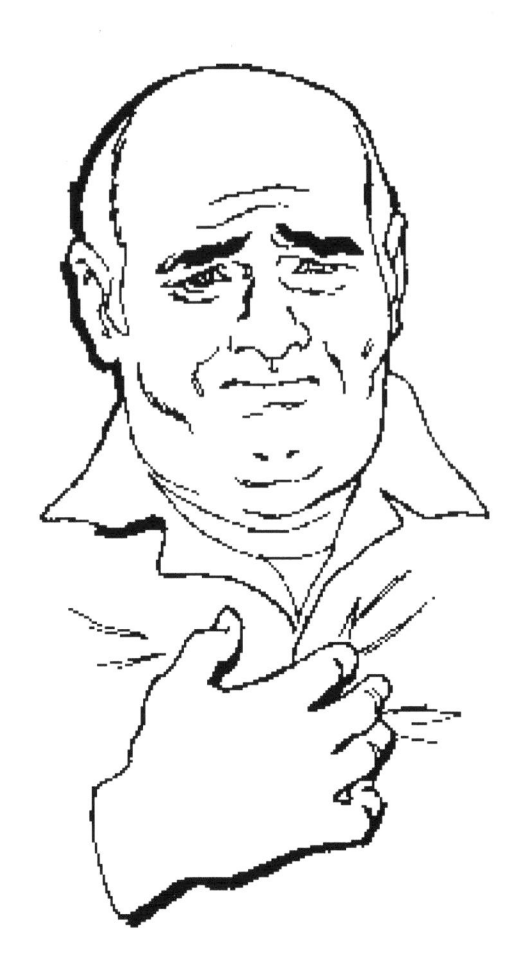

"What can I say .... this book's like true love – it kinda gets you right here."

The Indian in the hills was sending smoke signals to his brethren in the valley below.

"What does the message say?" a visitor to the Reservation asked the chief.

"I'm not sure," the chief retorted, "I believe he is telling us that his blanket is on fire."

What is the longest word in the English language? Smiles. there is a mile between the first and last letters.

Every time I give him a banana, he goes ape.

After a lengthy psychiatric examination, the doctor called the little boy's mother into his office for consultation.

"So does my little boy have an inferiority complex?" the mother asked.

"No," replied the doctor, "he *is* inferior."

Mary had a little lamb,
Little lamb, little lamb.
Mary had a little lamb,
The doctor was amazed.

Armageddon: the time when Armageddon outta here!

Dejected Lover: "She stole my heart."
Listener: "I guess we can have her arrested for petty theft."

First Secretary: "Your boss sure keeps you busy."
Second Secretary: "You've got that right. He dictates eighteen to twenty letters a day. Sometimes even twice that."
First Secretary: "Wow. He sure is a real dictator."

A businessman was asked by his company to attend a convention of computer peripheral suppliers in New York City. Noting that the event was to span three days, he planned his after-hours entertainment as well as sightseeing, remembering how much New York City had to offer.

While he packed his clothes, an old ticket fell out of the drawer.

"Amazing," he said out loud, "this is a shoe repair claim check from 1942. How in the heck did this ticket stay hidden all these years?"

As he looked at the claim check, memories of his Army leave

in New York in 1942 came back. It was a whirlwind, wild time for a young small-town boy.

"Those shoes. I completely forgot about them," he reflected, "I was on leave and the ship was departing and I had to rush to the port, abandoning those shoes. They were great shoes; black with shiny, white-tipped toes, brass fasteners along the sides....many good times wearing those shoes."

He placed the claim check in his wallet and flew off to the Big Apple. After arriving he settled into his swank hotel room and checked his schedule.

"I have some time to kill tomorrow, maybe I'll see if that old shoe repair shop still exists," he thought.

The next day he took a cab to the address on the claim check and to his great surprise the old shoe repair shop was still there. It looked a lot more weathered and battered than his mind's eye recollection, but there it was, nonetheless. He wondered if the original owner was still operating the shop.

The businessman went inside and rang the bell on the counter. A very old man came out from behind a curtain in back of the counter area.

"This may sound ridiculous," the businessman started, "but I recently found this old claim check for .... well, uh.... you see I left these shoes here for repair in 1942. Do you think it is possible that these shoes are still here?"

The old man took the claim check and said, "We will see." He then went out behind the curtain.

About ten minutes later the old man emerged from the back of the shop, went over to the businessman and said, "They'll be ready Tuesday."

The mathematician-turned-philosopher traveled to the big city where he studied the mean and standard deviate.

A doctor is awakened in the middle of the night by gurgling sounds emanating from his bathroom.

He rushes into the room, turns on the light and discovers, to his horror, that not only is his drain clogged, but his faucet can't be shut off. Water is beginning to flow over the edge of the sink. The doctor frantically dials the number of his plumber.

"You've got to come over and help me," he stammers.

"It's a little like what you always tell me," the plumber says calmly. "Throw two aspirins down the drain and call me in the morning."

Lions travel in prides, cattle travel in herds, birds travel in flocks, and cars travel in clogs.

*Remember the hippies of the late 1960's? They wore beards and torn jeans and smoked pot. Now they are businessmen and the so-called mainstream society now looks just like what we made fun of back then. Well, let's look briefly back down memory lane.*

First Hippie: "Hey, man. Turn on the radio."
Second Hippie: "Radio. I love you."

Visitor to San Francisco's Haight Ashbury district: "Do you hippies believe in free love?"

Hippie: "Sure man. Like, who has money?"

Two hippies were traveling by car along the highway when they arrived at a hidden intersection.

"Tell ya what, man," the driver said, "you look to your side as I pull forward and tell me if anything is coming. I'll look my way."

He pulled forward about ten feet and asked, "Well, see anything?"

The passenger replied, "Nothing but a dog."

The driver then began to drive through the intersection. Suddenly there was a tremendous crash.

The two hippies awoke in the hospital the next morning. They dazedly looked at each other and the driver collected his thoughts.

"Hey, man," the driver complained, "you said there was nothing coming but a dog."

The other hippie said, "Yeah. A Greyhound."

"Waiter, come here" the diner screamed, "what's this fly doing in my soup?"

The waiter looked into the soup and said, "Looks like the backstroke."

Joe: "When are you going to junk this heap?"
Fred: "Heap? This is a perfectly good car."
Joe: "Oh, yeah? Explain the buzzards circling overhead."

Frustrated mother to her teenage son: "I suppose if your friends told you to jump off a bridge, you would."

Teenage son: "Not again, I wouldn't."

Semiconductor: the driver of a tractor trailer.

Dan: "I love bacon. It makes up an important part of my diet."
Ann: "You mean you actually need bacon?"
Dan: "It satisfies my need for red meat."

"U-u-u-r-r-p!" The cannibal belched vociferously.

"What's wrong?" a cannibal sitting next to him asked.

"I seem to be full of gas," he said. "I must have eaten a politician."

A shipping department clerk decided to save a little time and loaded up his arms with boxes. Barely able to see over the top box, he started to walk down the aisle.

Another clerk, noticing that the man's arms were completely occupied, called out, "Got a match?"

"Not since Superman," came the reply.

With world crises ever expanding, the Pope decided that he must present his views on hope, love and peace in a more determined manner. He prepared himself for an extended journey and his staff made travel and lodging plans across thirty countries on four continents.

In all, the mission was to last just over six weeks.

After his arrival back at the Vatican, the Pope planned to speak to the people the next morning.

Arising early, the Pope was astonished to see that Saint Peter's Square was literally packed with people awaiting his presence.

When he stepped out onto the balcony, the huge crowd shouted in unison, "Long time, no See."

The man suffered from tired blood. When he cut his hand, it bled a week later.

The traveler was weary; he stopped at the first hotel he came across. Though the establishment looked rather shopworn, he entered the building and went up to the front desk.

"Do you have reservations?" the clerk asked him.

"Yes, I do," answered the traveler, "But I want to stay here anyway."

Mystery: Mr. Tery's sister.

The circus came rumbling into town with all of the expected regalia. The march of the elephants stirred the children's excitement and crowds of youngsters ran and danced along with the wagons full of animals.

Acrobats performed their routines alongside the wagons and the clowns beckoned one-and-all to come out to the grand opening that Saturday.

On Saturday the overflow crowd pushed its way into the huge tent. Outside, one straggler decided to take one more look at the shows behind the tent. There in the elephant cage he spotted an old friend of his from many years back.

"Herbert!" the man shouted. "Is it really you?"

"Jack!" Herbert cried out. "How have you been? I haven't seen you in over fifteen years."

"So. what have you been doing with yourself these past fifteen years?" Jack asked.

"Just what you see here, cleaning the elephant cage," he retorted.

"I've been working knee deep in elephant waste for more than a third of my life," Herbert laughed. "I even know all the elephants by sight and name."

"How can you even stand it?" Jack questioned him, looking at the mounds of mess spread across the cage floor.

"I can't, really," Herbert complained.

"Why don't you quit, then?" Jack demanded.

Herbert answered, sighing, "You know how it is. I'd quit in a minute, except I would hate to leave show business."

Bill: "Have you ever heard a rubber band?"
Will: "Sure. In fact, I played in one once."
Bill: "Was the music difficult?"
Will: "No. It was a snap."

Husband: "Yow. Look at that! My hairline is really receding."
Wife: "No it's not."
Husband, smoothing his hair back with his hand, "Yeah? What do you call this?"
Wife: "Your face is growing through your scalp."

Then there was the pig that had laryngitis. He walked away disgruntled.

A peanut sat on the railroad track. It's heart was all aflutter. Along came a train going clickitty-clack. Toot! Toot! Peanut butter.

Bob: "How come hurricanes are named after women?"
Jill: "Because if they were named after men, they would be called 'himacrutches.'"

Novocain: a support aide for an old Chevrolet Nova.

The wealthy man was hounded by his wife until he finally went with her to make out his will.
She knew that where there was a will, there was a way.

Banjo: don't let Joe in this joint.

Two drunks were walking along a railroad track. The track was straight as an arrow and went on for as far as the eye could see.
First Drunk: "Man, these stairs seem to go on forever."
Second Drunk: "I don't care about the steps; it's these darned low railings that are killing me."

Mesopotamia: a whole lot of potamia.

Elephant to zoo keeper: "I quit!"

Zoo keeper: "Why are you quitting? Don't we treat you well?"

Elephant: "Oh the living quarters are all right, I guess; but you're paying me peanuts."

Anthony was a simple man. He was kind to everyone he met and he asked nothing in return. But poor Anthony had little money, barely enough to support his simple lifestyle.

One day he met a priest who felt immediate sympathy for this man of such goodness, but of such poverty.

"I have only a little bit of money, but I would be happy to give it to the Church," Anthony told the priest.

The priest answered him, "The Church accepts money only from those who can afford it. But it is the good deed that is far and away more important than any monetary contribution. Why don't you come and live in the little caretaker's house behind the church?"

Anthony accepted on the condition that he be allowed to work for his keep. They shook hands on the agreement and Anthony began his duties at the church the next morning.

Anthony proved to be a tireless worker and he worked virtually around the clock. He not only cleaned the church and the grounds, he helped those in need in the community of any religion. He painted houses, shopped for the elderly, read to the blind.

Anthony's great spirit and kindness came to the attention of the church elders and he was offered the chance to become a priest. The local Diocese paid all expenses and within just two years Anthony was ordained as a priest.

Still his tireless efforts continued. In fact, it seemed as though Anthony worked harder than ever. The community leaders honored him in every way they could for his great civic responsibility.

Anthony received honors within the Church as well and he was soon ordained as Bishop.

The honors only seemed to inspire Anthony to work even harder. It was difficult to imagine any human being carrying his work load and bearing his work ethic. He seemed tireless with an enormous capacity to bring joy and happiness.

The Vatican soon came to recognize just how important a man Anthony was not only to the Church, but to the communities he worked in and visited.

Anthony rapidly was promoted to Archbishop and then Cardinal. This great man who had so selflessly worked for the good and benefit of others was notified through the "official" rumor mill that he was now up for the highest honor the Church could offer: the Pope.

The decision was unanimous and Anthony was named Pope. He was visibly shaken by the enormity of the honor, for this simple man from a simple background had never forgotten his roots.

He was called before the Vatican Council to receive his honor. He slowly walked to the large, ornate room where the Council members eagerly awaited his entrance. The now old man stepped before the Council and made his announcement.

"I am so greatly honored by your electing me to the Papacy," Anthony said, his eyes moist from tears of joy. "But I must tell you that all of my life I have worked hard, very, very hard for the good of others. I have worked long hours all of my life and I worked ever harder as I rose through the ranks to this honor you have bestowed upon me today."

Anthony looked around the room at the eager faces. He then said, with sadness in his heart, "I must respectfully decline this great honor. I simply cannot perform the necessary duties."

With tears now streaming down his cheeks he declared, "I am just too pooped to Pope."

Congress: a great vacuum into which all money is drawn.

A man walks into the psychiatrist's office with a pelican standing on the top of his head.

"Doc, you've gotta help me," the pelican shouts, "Get this man off my feet."

A man sitting near the back of the restaurant was puffing on a most vile smelling, smoky cigar.

The waitress accosted him, "Sir, you can smoke that cigar if you don't bother the lady diners."

"I'd rather bother the lady diners," he replied.

Cucumber: "I had a hard childhood."
Tomato: "Why? What happened?"
Cucumber: "My father never paid attention to me. He would come home pickled."

The father was visibly upset with his teenage daughter, when he found out that she was pregnant.

"Was it your current boyfriend, Gary?" the father demanded.

"No," the girl cried, it wasn't Gary."

"I know," said the father, "it was that low-down scum ball, Leo. How many times have I warned you to stay away from Leo?"

"I haven't seen Leo in ten months," she cried harder.

"If it wasn't Gary and it wasn't Leo, then who was it then?" the father shouted.

"No one," she sobbed.

"It had to be someone, you just couldn't have a baby out of thin air!" the father roared, and he began quickly pacing back and forth.

"I'm telling you," the whimpered, "there was no one, no one at all."

"It's a miracle!" the father screamed sarcastically, "We are going to witness the Virgin Birth!"

Bricklayer: a very painful occupation for a chicken at a construction site.

Soothsayer: a man who says the sooth, the whole sooth and nothing but the sooth.

The elderly woman opened her refrigerator door and a little voice called out, "Please close that door."
She looked and looked and discovered that the little voice was coming from a jar of vinegar and oil.
"Why should I close the door?" she asked politely.
"Can't you see I'm dressing?" the jar responded.

The little ink drop was so sad. His father was sent to the pen and the sentence was long.

It has been said that London swings. Then is it true that Brussels sprouts?

The lone jackal wandered aimlessly through the jungle growth, scavenging for food.
He traveled out from the tree line, across the breadth of the open plains and into the foothills. Once in the hills, the weather slowly began to change.
First the change was subtle, with the winds blowing just a little harder each day. Soon the temperature noticeably dropped. The colder days combined with the stronger winds caused great deal of discomfort for the jackal.
The poor critter sought shelter, but a satisfactory escape from the weather was not at hand. The wind and the cold continued on in their menacing onslaught.
The next day he came upon a dead water buffalo. The jackal

slowly walked around the huge carcass. He soon realized that here was enough meat and skin to satisfy his needs for both food and shelter.

Over the following few days, the lone scavenger made a wonderful coat out of the skin of the water buffalo. Now sheltered from the icy elements, the wild dog proudly trotted out from his hiding place.

As he passed a small group of hunters, one of the hunters gasped, and then screamed, "A-a-a-h-h-h! It's jackal and hide!"

The pilot was heading the plane sharply upward. The copilot was growing more and more concerned that the plane would soon fly above its acceptable range.

"What's your beef?" the pilot snapped at him.

"Hey," the copilot shot back, "I don't like your altitude."

Dale: "Wow, that new Rock band sure brought the house down."

Gale: "They were that good, huh?"

Dale: "Not really. They just tore the supports out."

Then there was the pig that tried out for the football team. He had to quit after he pulled a hamstring muscle.

Tangible: a tan dirigible.

The newly married husband bought his wife a fur wrap for her neck as a token of his love.

"This is a mink stole, isn't it?" she asked cutely.

"Hey. I bought that fair and square," he scolded her.

If it stands to reason,
Does it sit to argue?

The young man arrived from a foreign country and could not speak one word of English. He went to live with his uncle who managed to get him employment with a local construction company.

"Just stay by me and do as I ask you and you will be all right," the uncle lectured the lad.

The first day on the job proceeded smoothly. The only problem was lunch: the young man did not bring his and ended the day hungry.

As the days passed, the work effort became easier and easier. He became almost an old hand at the job. The uncle was beaming his pride at his nephew.

Unfortunately, lunch remained a problem. Unable to speak English, the nephew could not eat at the local restaurants.

"Teach me a lunch meal I can order," the frustrated lad asked his uncle one day.

"OK. Repeat after me: 'apple pie and coffee .... apple pie and coffee,'" the uncle said repeatedly and each time his nephew mimicked the words.

The next work day brought a newly confident young man to the construction site. At the sound of the lunch whistle, he proudly walked into the restaurant across the street.

"What can I get you?" the waitress behind the counter asked him.

With a broad smile on his face, the lad said in a firm voice, "Apple pie and coffee."

It worked! This was the first lunch the young man had enjoyed, since joining the construction crew.

The days turned into weeks and the nephew became a regular. Soon the waitress would bring out the order without even asking him first. But, alas, too much of anything can become overbearing, and especially if that anything is apple pie and coffee.

"I am fed up to here with apple pie and coffee," the nephew complained, placing the side of his hand in front of his eyes. "I need something new."

The uncle thought of a simple, easy-to-say meal. "Say 'cheese sandwich,'" he instructed. The lad repeated after his uncle until he had mastered the new order. "Cheese sandwich," he said silently.

The following day our young man was ready, sitting at the counter with a broad smile on his face.

"What can I get you today?" the waitress asked him.

"Cheese sandwich," he declared, looking her squarely in the eye with confidence written all over his face.

"White or rye?" she asked pleasantly.

Confused, he suddenly yelped, "Apple pie and coffee!"

The bald eagle was proudly watching her nestling hatching. One by one the little pieces of the shell fell away.

The proud little American Eagle popped out of his remaining shell segment and cried out his first words: "E pluribus unum!"

The trash men were busy emptying the cans from both sides of the street. One of the men kept stopping and examining the contents of several of the trash cans. Every so often, he would remove an item and put it in a large pouch hanging by his side.

"What on earth are those things you're taking?" the truck driver asked him.

"They're collector's items," he responded.

Psychic: "I wandered into Ace's Grocery Store and inexplicably felt myself being forced to buy every brand of chocolate cake, cookie, pie, pudding and milk mix the store had."

Friend: "Very strange. Do you know why it happened?"

Psychic: "I'm not sure. I really don't know whatever possessed me."

Taxidermist: a cab driver that literally scares you out of your skin.

Purple Heart: a military award received when you pound your chest.

Teacher: "Ben, you cheated on your homework book report, didn't you?"
Ben: "Well, I....uh...."
Teacher: "Tell me the truth."
Ben: "I can't."
Teacher: "Why not?"
Ben: "Because I will get Billy Roberts in trouble."

Humble: a bull that never knows the words to a song.

Boxer in the corner: "How am I doing so far?"
Manager: "Great. You're wearing him out on your face."

The farm boy looked on in amazement as the cows began jumping over a flattened portion of fencing. As they charged forward, the pigs rushed to face them.

A battle ensued. The cows knocked over pigs and tried to step on them. The pigs rolled under the cows, hitting their legs, sending the big beasts tumbling.

Soon the chickens joined the fray, screeching and scratching at the cows and pigs..

The sheep were next. The battlefield became so crowded no one could tell who was fighting whom and who was winning or who was losing.

The boy was frozen in his place by the magnitude of the battle. He was dumbfounded as to why this fracas started in the first place.

The farmer looked out of his window and rushed outside in horror.

"What in the blue blazes is going on out there, boy?" the farmer screamed in panic.

"It's a food fight!" the boy responded.

"Food fight .... maybe my food is fighting against this book .... that's it!

Jack: "Did you here that Ruth is leaving the company?"
Mack: "Oh, no! That's terrible news."
Jack: "Why?"
Mack: "We'll be ruthless!"

Chemistry: a family lineage that shows that all of your ancestors were chemists.

We live in a military society: We have General Chaos, Major Crises, Corporal Punishment and Private Parts.

Level headed: someone with a truly flat head.

Then there was the jazz musician who also ran a company that solicited public opinion. He was a poll cat!

Mother to her college-bound son: "Do you think you will be able to join the University Chorus next year?"
Son: "I hope so, if I can get enough glue."

Zanuck: "That music that you were just playing. Was it Chopin? Was it Beethoven?"
Arturo: "I don't know. It was Grieg to me."

Wife: "Honey, did you get the tickets for the play, like I told you to do?"
Husband: "Of course I did. Can't you trust me to do anything?"
Wife: Well, where in the theater are the seats located?"
Husband: "Over to the side, I guess."
Wife: "Over to the side? How far over *are* the seats?"
Husband: "I'm not sure, but the ticket agent said he'd leave the window open so we could see the stage."

Then there was the frustrated man who rushed downtown to the big department store because he saw a large newspaper ad that read: "Women's clothing 50% off!"

The famous critic was in town for a convention of his ilk. Knowing that he was there, the local symphony invited him to their concert that evening.

"We are giving a World Premiere of an orchestra/chorus work written by our local composer," the symphony manager told him. "We would be most honored if you could attend the evening's festivities."

"I will make every effort to attend," the critic said.

The evening arrived and the critic took his prize guest box seat overlooking the stage. The concert rambled onward until the grand moment for the World Premiere arrived.

The orchestra and the chorus melded, diverged, counterpointed each other. The musicians played and the conductor conducted with great fury.

The piece, *Grand Symphony of 1000*, played on for a full forty five minutes. All the time the composer kept glancing at the critic to see his reaction.

The finale crescendo filled the hall with the sounds of singers and musicians trying to top one another for volume.

After the concert ended all the special guests were invited to a reception, wherein the composer was introduced to the critic.

"Well, how did you like the piece?" the composer asked.

"It was, ah, interesting," the critic answered, picking his words carefully. "I especially liked the finale."

"Oh, you found the chords and words and the orchestrations exciting?" the composer eagerly inquired.

"No. It was because I knew it was finally over," the critic responded.

Dan: "I donated my brain to science."
Larry: "You mean archeology."
Dan: "Why archeology?"
Larry: "They'll have to dig deep to find it."

Some people have to stand up to think better. It takes the pressure off the brain.

Chuck: "I heard Marty had a terrible fall. How is he?"
Dick: "The doctor says he has water on the brain."
Chuck: "That's an improvement. It used to be alcohol."

A French dog has *bon appétit.*

A man was taking the written portion of the examination for his driver's license.
Question #4: "Who has the right of way when four cars arrive simultaneously at a four-way stop sign?"
After much thought he wrote: "The pickup truck with the gun rack and the bumper sticker saying, 'Guns don't kill people. I do.'"

World's smartest scientist: Einstein....second smartest: Zweistein.

Perfume: an aroma used by women to attract men.
Car fume: an aroma used by cars for the same reason.

Judge: "This is the fourth day in a row that you have been arrested for public drunkenness. When will this stop?"
Drunk: "When I can see my way straight."

Reminder sign on barbarian leader's bedroom wall: "Remember, pillage THEN burn."

It's recently been discovered that research causes cancer in rats.

Clairvoyant: Mr. Voyant's unusually perceptive wife.

A man was taking the oral portion of the examination for his driver's license. The examiner opened the test book and asked the first question.
Examiner: "What does a yellow light mean?"
Man: "It means you had better speed up, because the light is going to turn red soon."

Sage advice: Be nice to your kids, for they will choose your nursing home.

On the church bulletin board there was the announcement for the coming event. It read: "Evening service tonight will be held at 6:30. The sermon topic will be 'What is hell?' Come early and listen to our choir practice."

Bank clerk: "Is this check good?"
Customer: "Good? Why, it's made out of the finest rubber money can buy."

Shin: A device designed specifically for finding furniture in the dark.

Two old men meet for the first time in twenty five years. After a short period of adjusting to their new looks, they begin conversation.
Rufus: "So tell me, Sol. How have the past twenty five years treated you?"
Sol: "Remember, Rufus, how, when I came home, my wife used to bring me the newspaper? How she would bring me my slippers? And my little dog would bark at me and chase me around the house?"

Rufus: "So how have things changed?"

Sol: "Now my new little dog brings me the newspaper. He brings me my slippers. But my wife! She follows me around the house barking at me about this....barking at me about that!"

Rufus: "What's your complaint? You're getting the same service."

A psychic is someone who is not too big and not too small. He or she is just a medium.

".... so, you still with me? Keep plugging, there's a light at the end of the tunnel – *u-u-r-p* – I sure hope the light's still on in the bathroom."

Boss: "Where's your husband?"
Wife: "He's calling in sick."
Boss: "He can't call in sick. He's used up all of his sick days."
Wife: "So he's calling in dead."

Two men conversing at the big school dance.
Bill: "Boy, Hal, you sure are a wall flower."
Hal: "I'd rather be a wall flower than a blooming idiot."

Dentist: a really poor driver.

*Now take a deep breath, plant your feet firmly on the ground, lean forward and let's burst toward the finish line. Just watch out for the mines.*

Sergeant: "Yo, Private Smith. I want you to move out straight ahead and when you get up to that ridge about 1000 feet to the left, signal me." Smith then jumped over the barbed wire fence and dashed out into the field.
Lieutenant: "Hey, Sarge. How do know where all the mines are placed?"
Sergeant: "That's what I'm finding out now."

The private shipping company was awarded a lucrative contract to lay mines in the enemy harbor.
"I think I'll take this opportunity to illegally collect some insurance," the company CEO mused to his trusted VP.
"How, so?" the VP queried.
"Well, I'll lay the mines in strategic zones that will interfere with my own shipping, so I can claim the losses."
"I see," replied the VP, "you are going mine your own business."

Herb: "The Coal Company gave me my own leg of a mine."
Jim: "I get it. They gave you the shaft."

The admiral saw three men floating in the water, apparently drowning. They seemed to be shouting, but no sound came out at all.

"Ensign Harmon," the admiral screamed, "over here on the double!"

"What is the problem, Sir?" Harmon asked.

The admiral screamed again, "I told you to start throwing the *mines* overboard....the *mines*"

Teacher in the class on nutrition: "Is it true that fish is good for the brain?"
Student: "Yeah, it's food for thought."

Sign on fraternity door: Beauty is in the eye of the beer holder.

Dentist: "It seems your teeth are just fine, Mrs. Jarrod."
Mrs. Jarrod: "Oh, that's certainly great news. I was so worried about them."
Dentist: "But I'm afraid your gums are going to have to be removed."

Employee: "You're two-faced!"
Boss: "I'm surprised you can count that high."

The tree nursery arrived at the construction site to plant two large trees. The trees were so large that only one could fit on a truck.

"I'll back this truck up to the fence line and get this poplar in place," one worker said to the other.

"The poplar doesn't go there," the second worker told him. "The oak goes there. I'll back the oak into place."

"You've got that all wrong," the first worker scolded him. "The tree that should be backed into place is the poplar. It makes so much more sense to put a poplar in that location."

"What's going on here?" the foreman chimed in, after hearing this conversation.

"Which tree goes over by the fence line?" the second worker asked him.

The foreman looked at the plans and then commented, "The oak, of course."

"See?" the second worker chided the first one, "I *told* you that you were backing up the wrong tree."

Every morning is the dawn of a new error.

The woodwind player was told by the conductor that he always played sour.

"You must do something about this," the conductor complained.

One day he brought a bottle of vinegar and a packet of herbs to the concert. He mixed the ingredients in a bowl and then began soaking his instrument in it.

"What's that for?" the conductor demanded.

"You have always complained that I play my piccolo sour, right?" the woodwind player complained.

"So?" the conductor replied.

"Now I'll have a dill piccolo," he retorted.

The new variety show on television featured a band made up of twenty violins and twenty saxophones, including eight alto, eight tenor, and four baritone saxophones.

After two weeks, however, the show was canceled. The viewers wrote in complaining that there was too much sax and violins.

Then there was the microbiologist whose exercise routine included twenty minutes a day of anaerobics.

Monkey National Anthem: "The Star-Spangled Banana."

The young man was trying to impress his new girlfriend with his deep sense of chivalry.

"I'd do anything for you," he began. "I'd crawl through mud for you. If I had to I would swim through the slimiest, most foul water to be by your side. I'd throw my finest coat into the street, to allow you to walk over it so you wouldn't get even so much as a speck of dirt on yourself. I'd even eat worms under torture if it meant I could be with you."

The next night the lad called the young lady to ask her for a date.

"I can't," she told him.

"But why not?" he pleaded.

"I think you are a really nice guy," she responded, "but you have such disgusting habits."

Polka: how to receive a slap.

Puppet to his master: "I'm quitting!"

Master: "First of all, where are you going to go? Anyway, I've told you many times that when I do well, so will you."

Puppet: "That's the whole trouble. You keep stringing me along."

The young musician was an idealist. He truly believed that music held the beauty that could charm the world. He began his quest in the deep jungles of Africa.

Stopping at a water hole, he looked around for animals. "This will be a good spot to present my demonstration," he said to himself. "Many animals of all types will pass this way."

As dusk started to spread over the land, the musician took his violin from its case and began to play. "Music hath charms that soothe the savage beast," he had always been told by his teacher. Here was the perfect setting to find out.

The beautiful, soft music floated from his violin like the wonderful aroma of the sweetest flowers. He played on and on, and the music became ever more beautiful. The melodies just soared in rapturous harmonies.

An antelope peeked out from around the dense brush and slowly walked toward the musician. There it lay down a few feet away, with a serene look on its face, mesmerized by the sheer beauty of the sound.

More antelopes and several water buffalo joined the first animal, enjoying the wonders coming from the violin.

Hyenas, wildebeests, ocelots, then tigers and crocodiles came forward. None of the animals displayed even the slightest animosity toward each other and especially toward the musician.

Hunters and the hunted all lay in close proximity, mesmerized by the music.

"It's so beautiful," the crocodile told a toucan.

"It's truly the most wonderful sound I have ever heard," the tiger purred.

Love, harmony and peace flowed over everyone.

"My teacher was right," the musician thought serenely.

Suddenly a lion burst from the bushes behind the violinist and tore him to shreds.

"Why did you do that!" the animals shouted. "It was so beautiful."

The lion put its paw to its ear and said, "E-h-h-h-h-h?"

Teacher: "When a woman graduates from college she is called an alumna. What is a man called who graduates from college?"
Student: "An aluminum."

Just because you are paranoid does not necessarily mean someone is not out to get you.

The wealthy gentleman had just purchased a brand new Mercedes. He took possession of the beautiful car the next Saturday. With the weather so beautiful he decided to take the car for a drive on the country roads. The car purred to perfection to the great delight of its owner.

A few miles from the dealership a tractor lurched from behind a wall on a farm road and crumpled the passenger side front door and quarter panel.

"Great Scott! My new car!" the man shouted in anger.

The farmer stepped down from the tractor and looked at the damage to the car.

"Do you realize how much this car costs?" the wealthy man screamed. "I just picked this car up not twenty minutes ago."

"Well," the farmer said, "that's the way the Mercedes Benz."

History books record the reign of Maximilian, Emperor of Mexico from 1864 – 1867. The books do not, however, mention his much more well-known brother, Thanks.

Where did the dog go after his tail was accidentally cut off? He went to a retail store.

Even if you win the rat race, you are still a rat.

What is pirate corn? A buccaneer.

Then there was the man who had his ankles cut off in battle. He was defeated.

One day a peasant had wandered off the main path and onto the royal peanut farm. While walking where he did not belong, he fell into a large vat of peanut butter in process.

The royal caretaker came upon the scene and immediately summoned the guards who promptly arrested the peasant.

The peasant, still covered with peanut butter for evidence, was brought before the king.

"What have we here." the king asked his head guard.

"A sticky subject," the guard answered.

It has been said that clothes make the man. Clearly, naked people have little or no influence on society.

Newscaster: "Well, Hal, what's in store for us this weekend?"

Hal: "The Channel 29 Super Weather is telling us that we are going to have rain – and a lot of it."

Newscaster: "When can we expect this rain to end?"

Hal: "The Super Weather forecast tells us it's going to rain until it stops."

The rock climber decided to turn to climbing mountains. When his friend asked him why, he replied, "I wanted my career to reach new heights."

Why did the tiger chase the jack rabbit? He was in the mood for fast food.

Then there was the paint chemist who was emulsional over his work.

The owner of the large private corporation was making a presentation before the members of his Board of Directors.

A secretary opened the door slightly to see if the meeting had begun and she noticed that many of the members were looking around the room trying to occupy their attention. Some members were even beginning to doze off.

Just then a delivery man was walking passed and from his position he could see only the company owner speaking.

"Who's he," the delivery man asked.

"He's the Chairman of the bored," the secretary responded.

The leader of a "banana republic" was put on trial for crimes against his country.

He was found not guilty due to a hung jury.

A kosher hamster is called a beefster.

The woman swerved her car around the corner, went off the road and crashed head-on into a tree.

A police car happened to be parked directly across the street from the accident scene. The policeman rushed over to the woman and found her sitting in the car looking very angry.

"Are you all right, Mam?" the policeman asked her.

"I don't understand how this accident occurred," she retorted bruskly. "When I saw the tree, I blasted the horn. But it got in the way, anyway."

Gloria: "A-a-a-c-k! What's that spider doing on the ceiling?"
Mary: "Looks like a fancy eight-step."

At the end of any company Christmas party we have an excellent example of a potted plant.

Hal: "How is your friend doing with his hyena ranch?"
Joe: "He sold it."
Hal: "Why?"
Joe: "It was becoming the laughing stock of the county."

Two men were having a fierce fight in the park. A large crowd had gathered and all that the spectators did was watch and cheer. Some people even began taking bets.

A gentleman was passing by and he, too, started watching. He became outraged at the crowd reaction and the bloodletting that was occurring. He stepped into the fracas intent on breaking it up.

One of the fighters hit him, sending him sprawling.

"What happened to you?" a policeman asked, just arriving.

"I was hit by a guided muscle," the gentleman groaned.

Bill: "Who is that guy who just stepped on my toes?"
Will: "Him? He's my foot doctor."
Bill: "What's he doing? Drumming up his own business?"

A young stud-to-be spotted a beautiful girl standing alone at the local town social. She was absolutely stunning and he could not miss this opportunity. Deciding that the time was right, he moved over to her and began whispering in her ear.

"See Spot run," he murmured affectionately.

"What did you say?" the girl asked, bewildered.

He leaned toward her again and whispered in her ear, "Dick and Jane went to the store. Run, Spot, run."

"What are you doing?" she demanded.

"I'm just trying to make small talk," he confided.

Ode to the Toucan:
>If one can, toucan.
>If toucan, maybe one can't.

Then there was the tree surgeon who needed more variety in his work, so he branched out.

The visitor to the tropical island ran indoors and hid in the basement, when he heard that a tarantula rainstorm was approaching.

Two men meet in a downtown variety store. As they look through the merchandise one of the men, not finding what he wants, asks the other, "Is this a stationery store?"
The second man answers, "Of course it is. You don't feel it moving, do you?"

June was known as one of the nation's most desperate criminals. Though she was known by only a first name, she wreaked havoc wherever she went.
Each time the authorities caught her, she made a mockery of the prison system, easily escaping within two weeks from even maximum security institutions.
The director of the FBI was at his wits end. At a high level meeting of his top brass he asked for a rundown of June's latest crimes and escapes.
"She was captured in July of last year after robbing four banks in Oklahoma," his top aide read from the report. "She was captured in late August, but escaped in a bundle in a laundry truck two weeks later after overpowering two guards. She then robbed six service stations and nine more banks in four other states before her capture in October. She was out on the street within two days, after blowing up her jail cell."

"This is much worse than I could have ever imagined," the FBI director lamented, as he paced restlessly around the room.

"There's more," the aide went on. "She escaped two more times in November – once in Texas and once in California. In December she handily bolted from jails in Nevada, Oregon, Michigan, Ohio, Maryland and Rhode Island."

"I get the picture," the FBI director interrupted. "It seems that June is busting out all over."

Sam: "What's Larry doing these days?"
Bill: "He's got a job as a hang glider pilot."
Sam: "I see. His career is soaring."

Two friends go to the cemetery to pay respects to the late husband of one of them. They searched for a half hour with no luck.

"Harriet, are you sure he's here?" the first one asked.

"Of course he's here," Harriet retorted. "Don't you think I know where my own husband is buried?"

They searched on for nearly another hour, still to no avail.

"Harriet, he can't be here; we've been searching all morning."

"I tell you he's here," Harriet scolded here. "Aha! Here it is; here's his headstone."

"But Harriet, the stone says 'Here lies Mrs. Harriet Goldenrod,'" the friend said in surprise.

"I know that," Harriet answered, "I had him put everything in my name."

Then there was the man who used too sharp a razor for shaving and he lost face.

Bill: "Isn't there a Persian story about a man and a dinghy?"
Will: "Yeah, it's the 'Rubber Yacht of Omar Khayyam.'"

The play was a long and arduous one for the performers. It was immensely successful and had been playing for over a month.

One night, the actors were in especially high spirits, since a famous promoter was to be in the audience. They were giving it their all when suddenly one of the actors grabbed his chest and fell over.

"Is there a doctor in the house?" the stage manager shouted.

A doctor came forward and pronounced the man dead and then he informed the audience of the sad news.

An elderly woman in the upper balcony yelled to the doctor, "Give him some chicken soup!"

"Chicken soup?" the doctor shouted back. "The man is dead, lady! What good will *that* do?"

"Couldn't hurt," she hollered.

The visitor to Las Vegas decided to try his luck in one of the casinos. Amid the hustle and bustle of the clientele, he happened to see a little boy wandering among the gaming tables.

"Hey, little boy! Come here for a moment," he called. The boy worked his way over to the man who asked him how old he was.

"I'm eight .... the hard way," the boy replied.

How do ghosts get drunk? They drink *boo*ze.

The old bell ringer in the local monastery had reached retirement age and wanted to take advantage of the opportunity to enjoy his golden years. The advertisements went out to other regions as the townspeople moved quickly to help the monastery staff fill the position.

One day a rather odd individual arrived at the monastery gate and announced that he was interested in being the new bell ringer.

"Have you any experience in this field?" the monastery business manager asked the man.

"Well, not in the usual way," the man replied, "you see, I can ring the bell in a very unique way – I use my forehead."

"How do you do that?" the business manager wondered.

"Come up to the bell tower and I will demonstrate," the man said and they went up the long stairway to the tower's belfry.

Up in the tower the man walked slowly to the farthest corner he could find. He then lowered his head slightly and ran full force into the bell. At the last moment he snapped his head forward, hitting the bell with his forehead. An extraordinarily loud, but sonorous ring clamored out from the bell.

"Why, that's absolutely astounding," the business manager remarked. "Can you do that again?"

"Most certainly," the man asserted and he repeated the amazing feat. Again, the sound was extraordinarily loud, but sonorous. The interviewer was just as amazed the second time around.

"You are hired," the business manager told the man and he started to lead the man out from the tower and back to the office to discuss the particulars.

The man said, "Wait a minute, I want to show you something even more extraordinary." He then ran back into the tower perch. He moved to the farthest corner and started to rush towards the bell again.

Unfortunately, he lost his footing and fell over the railing to the ground ninety feet below.

The horrified residents who witnessed this tragedy ran to the man to help him, but it was hopeless. The poor man had perished in the fall.

The police arrived and cleared away the crowd, while the emergency medical team tried to revive the man.

The business manager sadly walked over to where the man was lying. One of the policemen asked him, "Do you know this man?"

"Not exactly," the business manager replied, "but his face rings a bell."

*And what do I do for the grand finale? Like the world, this book will end with a whimper.*

    Will: "Were you just talking to yourself?"
    Bill: "I don't know. I wasn't listening."

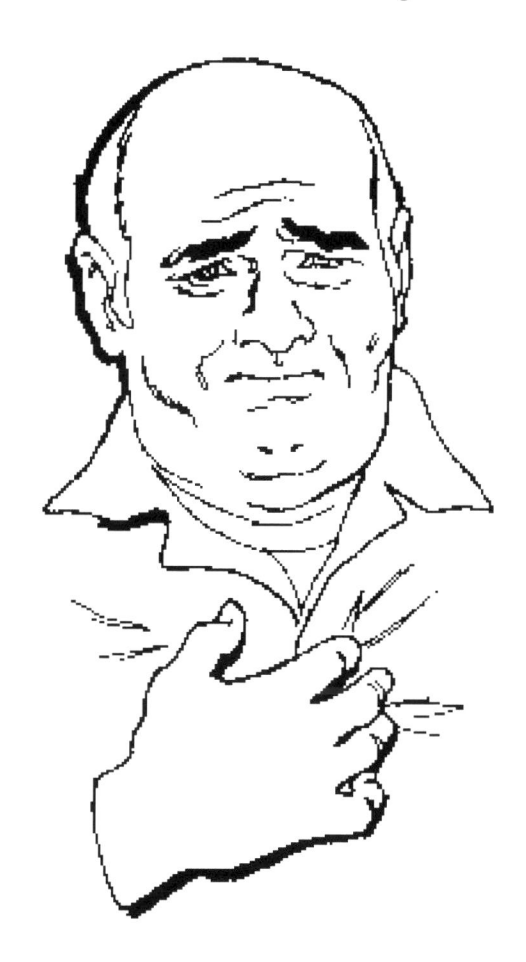

"Well, that about wraps this one up. And it certainly should be kept under wraps. I just hope you enjoyed this book as much as I – m-m-m-m-p-p-h, urp – did."

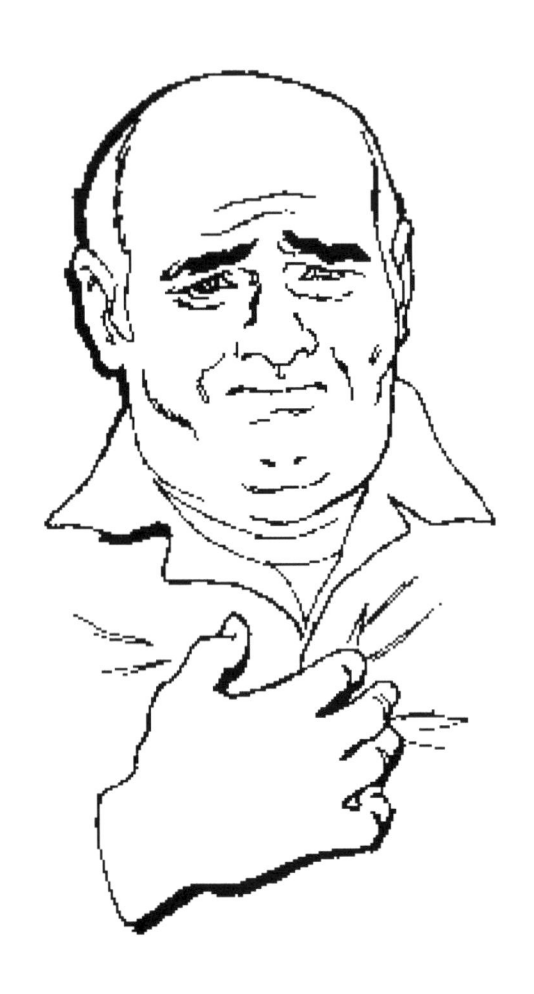

"Couldn't resist turning the page, could you? Hey, don't blame me .... I've been as much a victim as you. Now if you'll just close the book .... I can get a little shut-eye."

Printed in Great Britain
by Amazon